M000167590

ESSENTIAL FLAMENCO GUITAR

VOLUME 1

AN IN-DEPTH COURSE FOR ABSOLUTE BEGINNERS
TO MORE ADVANCED PLAYERS

BASIC TECHNIQUES
SOLEÁ
ALEGRÍAS

BY JUAN MARTÍN

Online Video

YouTube
www.melbay.com/30458V

Video
dv.melbay.com/30458

Visit us at www.melbay.com – E-mail us at email@melbay.com

Recordings, transcriptions, book by Patrick Campbell.

Photographs from Juan Martín's personal collection.

Video in NTSC 16:9 format.

The guitars played in the video are:
  Conde Hermanos, Madrid, 1974
  Gerundino Fernández, Almería, 1972
  Sobrinos de Esteso, Madrid, 1972 (peg-head)
  Conde Hermanos, Madrid, 1995
  Juan Miguel Carmona (negra), Granada, 1984
  Stephen Eden, Lewes, UK, 2011 (peg-head)

FLAMENCOvision
LONDON . MÁLAGA

P.O. Box 508
LONDON N3 3SY
UNITED KINGDOM

CONTENTS

INTRODUCTION by Juan Martín

Learning flamenco guitar should be a pleasurable voyage of discovery and developing skill, and I hope this program will help you enjoy that journey. I assume no prior knowledge of the guitar or of flamenco, so at the start of this first volume we need to devote time to the basics of the guitar and its playing techniques before we can get very far into the music. We start with music that is easy enough for the absolute beginner, yet is both authentic and interesting. I introduce essential techniques for the right and left hands, using simple examples of real flamenco to show these techniques in action. There are a few technical exercises, but not many, because the aim is to help you to start playing worthwhile music as quickly as possible.

The musical examples in this first section on techniques are from various *palos* – the Spanish term for the different rhythmic forms and song-styles of flamenco. The main discussion of these comes later, in this and subsequent volumes, when you have some familiarity with the basic techniques. Once that's achieved we can move on to a systematic discussion of the most important *palos,* emphasizing their rhythmic structure and impetus, demonstrating *falsetas* – the melodic passages – and giving some brief examples of the singing (the *cante*) and dancing (*baile*) to show something of the role of the guitar in the full flamenco experience. Even if, like very many guitarists, you are primarily interested only in playing solo guitar, some appreciation of the guitar's essential role in the *cante* and *baile* will help you to a much deeper understanding of the music. As you will hear me stress in the videos, mastery of the rhythmic pulse, the *compás*, is by far the most essential skill for any flamenco performer.

Today it's common to hear debates about the relative merits or otherwise of 'modern' flamenco and more traditional styles. The guitarist has to be first and foremost a musician and not just a follower of fashions. Flamenco is evolving and will continue to do so and, as in any musical tradition, there must be a place for novelty, for attempts at fusion with other musical genres *and* for respect for the historical roots of the tradition, which underpin everything that is unique and valuable about flamenco. My aim is to steer a course which embraces the fundamental values, the essential elements, of flamenco guitar playing in its many forms, so that you will meet traditional material as well as more 'modern' sounds. I have also ensured that there is minimal overlap in musical material between this and my other publications, so that even if you are a more advanced player you will find music that is unfamiliar and challenging enough to reward study and practice.

My two volumes of graded solos, entitled *Solos Flamencos*, published by Mel Bay Publications and each including access to an online video and audio recording, act as companion volumes to this program and provide a lot more music in many different *palos* to extend your repertoire.

I encourage all my students to hear and see as much flamenco as possible and to pay a lot of attention to the rhythmic pulse – the *compás* – and the emotional meaning of flamenco – the *aire* – rather than getting too carried away by the desire for ever greater speed and technical brilliance. Getting a real flamenco sound from the guitar is also very important. You will find that if you are looking for, and care about, the real essence of flamenco guitar, its musical soul, your instrument can begin to express it for you almost from the very start. Anybody who hears you play will be grateful, too!

I would particularly like to thank our publisher Collin Bay and his colleagues for their generous support and help and my dear friends, Raquel de Luna, Amparo Heredia, and Miguel Infante who, together with Carlos Brias, helped in the making of the videos.

¡Vamos a tocar!

Juan Martín.

KEY TO SYMBOLS AND NOTATION

NOTATION　The music is transcribed in both standard staff notation and guitar tablature *(cifra)*. For the sake of clarity, time-values of notes and details of fingering (other than *rasgueo* strokes) are indicated only in relation to the staff notation and have not been duplicated in the *cifra*.

FINGERING　Left hand fingering is indicated by numbers beside notes, with 0 denoting an open string and the fingers numbered 1 to 4, e.g. for an E major chord position: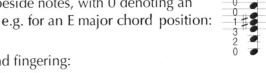

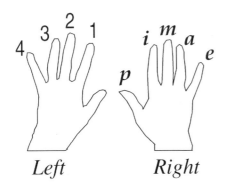

Left　　　*Right*

Right hand fingering:

p = thumb *(pulgar)*
i = index finger *(índice)*
m = middle finger *(medio)*
a = third finger *(anular)*
e = little finger *(meñique)*, in strummed *rasgueos*

POSITION　Ringed numbers beneath notes indicate string to be played: e.g. ⑤ . Roman numerals above the staff indicate fret positions relative to the capo *(cejilla)* or nut if no capo is used. **C** before a Roman numeral denotes a first finger *barré*, e.g **CV** means that the left index finger stops all six strings at the 5th fret. Small numbers written as a fraction before the **C** show the number of strings stopped by the first finger if the number is less than all six. Thus $^4_6$ **CV** indicates that the top four strings are stopped by the first finger.

CIFRA (TAB)　The six-line staff represents the six strings of the guitar with the first string at the top. Numbers on each line indicate the fret at which notes are played on that string, relative to the capo *(cejilla)* if the latter is used. **0** denotes open string.

RASGUEOS　*Rasgueos* are strummed strokes.

A down-stroke (towards the floor, from bass to treble) is indicated by an arrow pointing upwards on the page.

This is an up-stroke, from treble to bass. The arrows are drawn this way to show the order in which the strings are struck. The letter beneath each arrow in the notation and in the *cifra* shows the right hand finger which makes the stroke. The stroke of each finger is shown separately, in both the notation and the *cifra*. Time-values are shown in the notation. This allows an accurate representation of the rhythm in different forms of *rasgueo*. In the example *(right)*, for instance, the accents fall on beats 1 and 2. A slur above the staff notation and above the *cifra* links the strokes of a multiple-fingered *rasgueo*.

A double arrow indicates a stroke made with two fingers (**m** and **a**) simultaneously.

A wavy line before a chord indicates that it is played as an *arpegio* (the Spanish term for an arpeggio) from bass to treble, so that the strings sound one after the other.

Here the wavy line has an arrow and the letter **p** beneath it, indicating that the *arpegio* is played as a single stroke by the thumb from bass to treble.

Sometimes an *arpegio* chord with the thumb is preceded by a fast *rasgueo* with the fingers, for example *(right)*:

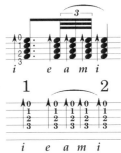

KEY TO NOTATION AND SYMBOLS (continued)

APAGADO   *Apagado* is a technique by which the sound of a chord is abruptly silenced by damping the strings with the right or left hand, immediately after a chord has been struck by a *rasgueo* stroke. When this is done by the left hand (sometimes also after single notes) the little finger is brought down lightly straight across the strings, thereby stopping them from sounding. When performed by the right hand the palm and palmar surface of the fingers stop the sound as the hand is slapped down across the strings.

Apagados are indicated in the notation and the *cifra* by a vertical bracket across the staff following the chord or note. Left hand *apagado* (*below left*) has a 4 above the bracket to indicate the 4th finger of the left hand.

        Right hand *apagado* has R above the bracket:

GOLPE   The *golpe*, a tap on the *golpeador* made with the ring finger, *a*, of the right hand (or sometimes with *a* and *m* together) is shown by a square symbol □ above the beat in both the notation and *cifra*. The tap may be made by itself or combined with an index finger or thumb down-stroke, as shown in the notation.

LIGADOS   A slur (a curved line) linking notes of different pitch indicates that the notes following the first note in the group are played only with the left hand by 'pulling off' (to sound a lower note) or by 'hammering on' (to sound a higher note), as in the example on the right.

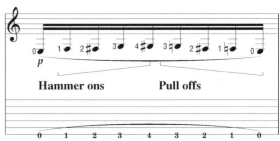

[Slurs for *ligado* are shown in both the notation and the *cifra*. A slur linking two notes of equal pitch, shown only in the notation, indicates that the time-value of the note first sounded should be prolonged by the duration of the second, following normal notational convention]

SLAPS   Slapping techniques are particularly characteristic of the Rumba rhythm. The first type you will see demonstrated is shown by the closed-fist symbol 👊 which indicates a slap on the strings with the backs of the fingers of the right hand, bent into a fist, stopping the vibration of the strings.

CONTINUAL RASGUEO   The 'continual' *rasgueo* is played by very rapid repetition of the four-stroke *rasgueo* (*e,a,m,i* consecutively and repeatedly). In this volume the many strokes of each finger are shown in the notation and the *cifra*.

Another form of continual *rasgueo* is played by repeated triplet *rasgueos*, notated on p.47 and illustrated on the video, Chapter 50.

   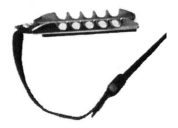

A traditional cejilla   *Jim Dunlop model*

TUNING THE GUITAR

The diagram (*below*) shows the way the six strings of the guitar are tuned. It also shows the fret positions at which notes of the next higher string are found, a valuable aid in tuning the guitar. Thus the note sounded at the fifth fret of the sixth string is the same note as that of the next higher string, the fifth string, A. The note at the fifth fret finds that of the next higher string for all the strings except the third string: here the note at the fourth fret sounds the same as the next higher string, the second string, B.

Strings

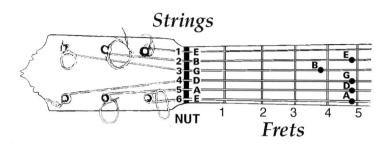

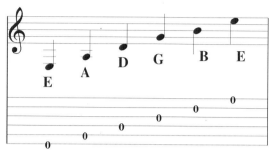

The notation and tablature on the right show the way the notes are written. By convention they are notated an octave higher than they actually sound on the guitar. On a piano the notes are found as shown below:

There are many possible ways of finding the notes to tune the guitar. Electronic tuners can now be obtained cheaply and in the video you will see an example of the vibration-sensitive type which is attached to the head of the guitar. These can be left in place during a performance, when it may otherwise be difficult to hear the notes. Simpler methods include the use of a tuning fork tuned to A (for the fifth string). Pitch pipes tend to be less reliable.

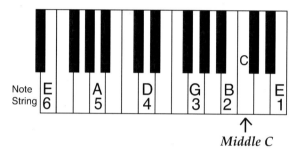

Once the strings have been tuned, further small adjustments may be necessary to ensure that the main chords of the piece to be played sound as they should.

In Spanish, the pitches of the notes are given different names. following the Spanish version of the tonic sol-fa system, as shown below.

Cuerdas

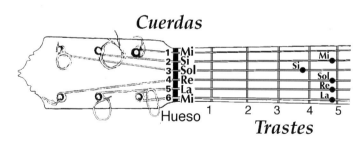

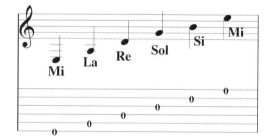

An example of a vibration-sensitive tuner

Note: In the video you will hear the string pitches named in English immediately followed by the Spanish. The second string is named as 'B or Si'. Si sounds like the English C, but the note is B.

BASICS

The video includes a sequence of four items (Chapters 2-5) which address the following topics:

    A. Holding the Guitar
    B. Peg-Head or Machine-Head Guitar?
    C. The Golpeador
    D. Care of the Fingernails

TWO CHORDS AND SIMPLE RHYTHMS

The first chord is E minor, so called because the third note of the E major scale is lowered (flattened) one semitone to make the minor chord. The second is called B7+E, because the B chord has the note A, seven letter steps above B, included. Here '+E' is added because the top E string is included in the chord to make it easier to play all six strings of the guitar at the beginning. The E does not strictly belong to a B7 chord. First, we see demonstrated simple down- and up- strokes, the down-strokes with the fingers *m* and *a* together, and the up-strokes with the thumb, *p*. The arrows may look the wrong way round, with the down-stroke pointing upwards on the page, but they are written this way to show the order in which the strings are sounded, from bass to treble.

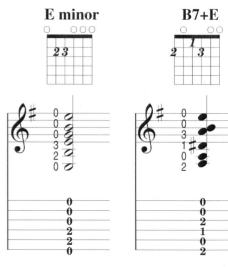

Chapter 1

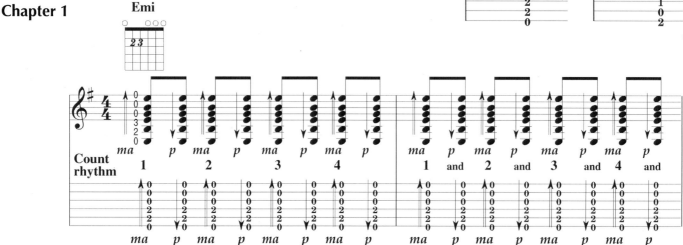

You can do quite a lot with these simple strokes, as is shown in a basic Rumba rhythm. What's important is the pattern of the rhythm, with the right accentuation: this rhythmic pattern is called the **compás**.

Chapter 6

First Rumba

(The following transcription is of the music introduced by 'If we were to take this a little faster . . .')

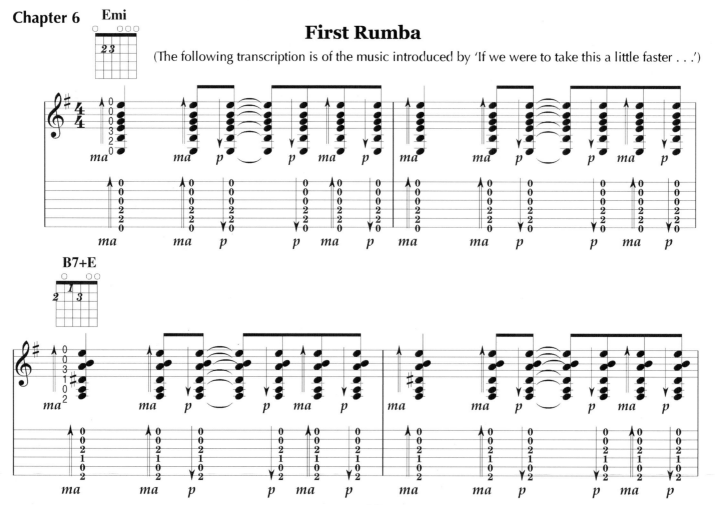

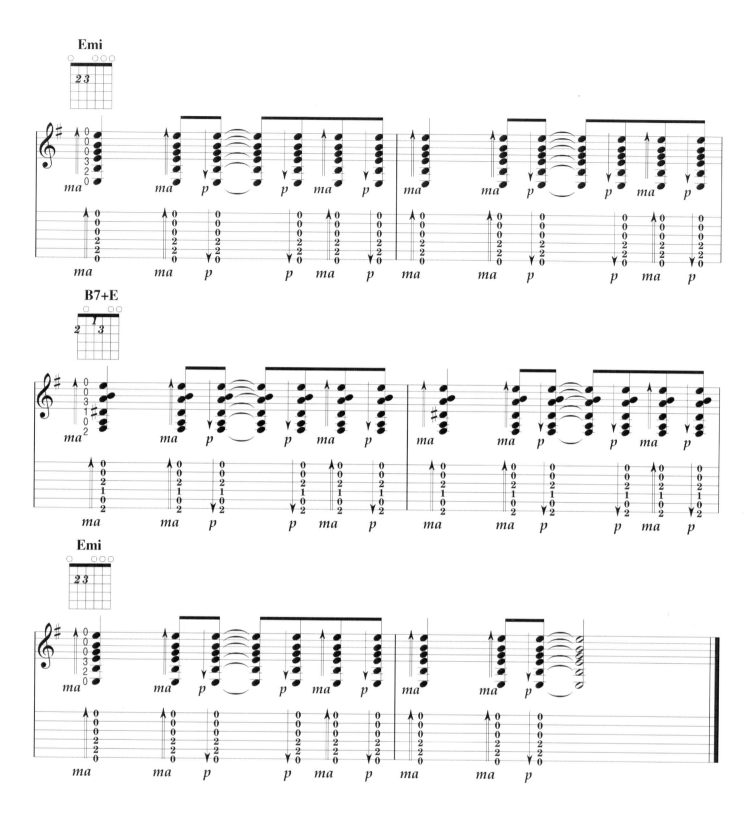

THE Ami7 CHORD

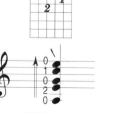

The next example of the Rumba rhythm with **ma** down-and **p** up-strokes, on the page following, includes the A minor 7th chord, which is written as shown on the left. This is an A minor chord including the seventh note of the A scale, G, in its 'natural' or unsharpened form. Only the top five strings are played, so **x** is written against the sixth string in the chord diagram to show that it is not sounded.

Minor seventh chords are heard often in flamenco today.

Simple Rumba with Ami7 chords (one bar to each chord)

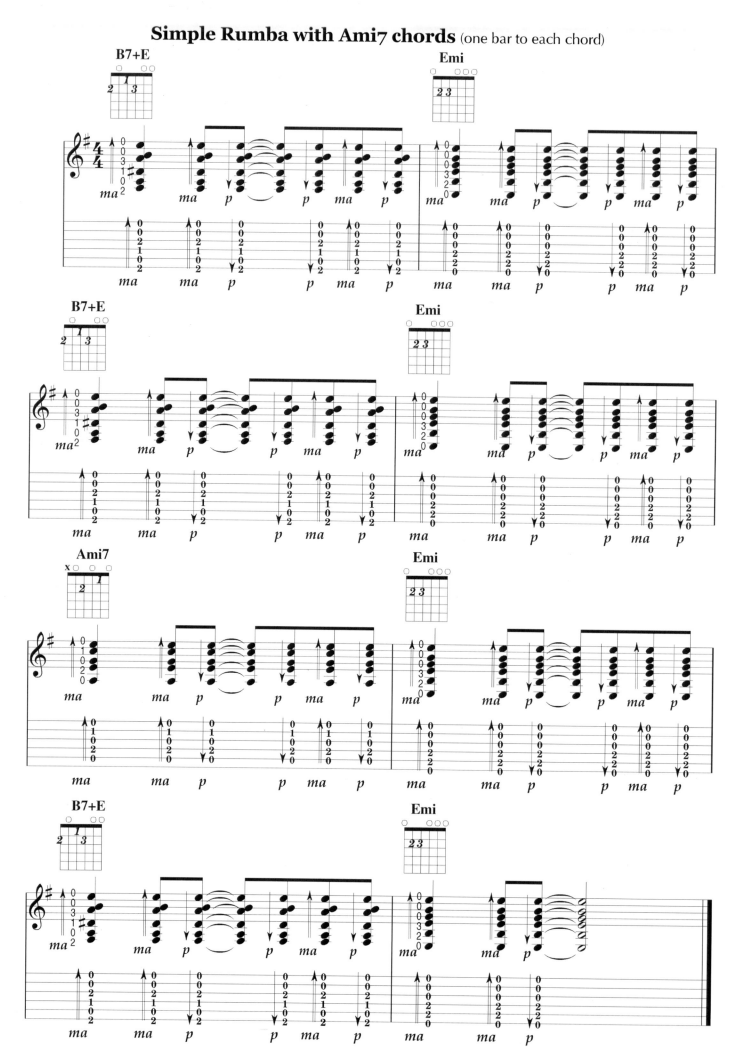

ALTERNATIVE SIMPLE RUMBA PATTERNS

These patterns use variations of the alternating down- and up-strokes. Two 4-beat bars are shown here.

Pattern B

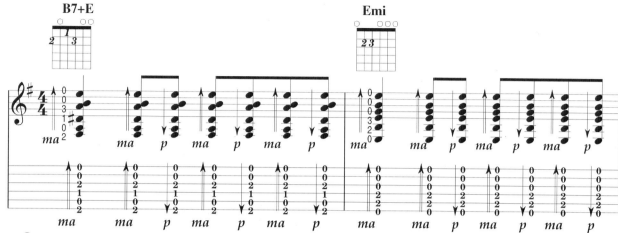

Pattern C

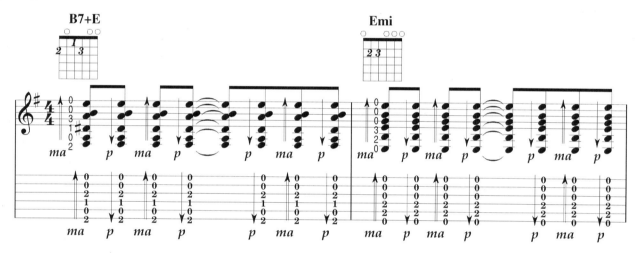

The 'more continuous' way of playing a basic Rumba rhythm shown in the video actually illustrates both the above two patterns, as it's so easy to slip between them. You could even play <u>all</u> the half beats with alternating down-strokes (*ma*) and up-strokes (*p*).

To summarize, this basic Rumba rhythm is made up of 8 half-beats, grouped 3:3:2, in each 4-beat measure, with accents on the first and fourth half-beats, which can be shown as follows:

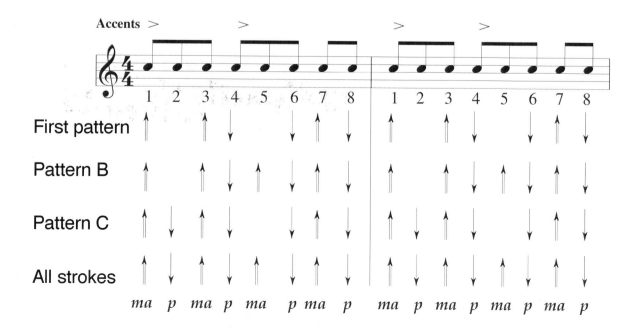

Chapter 8

Second Rumba, with 'Phrygian' Flamenco Chords

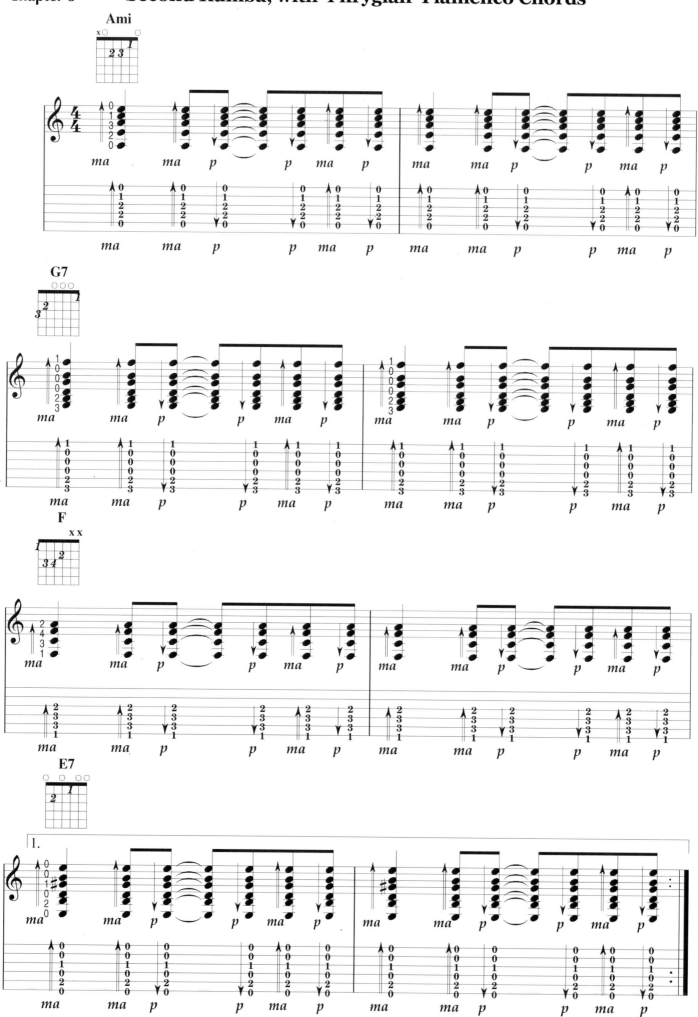

E major

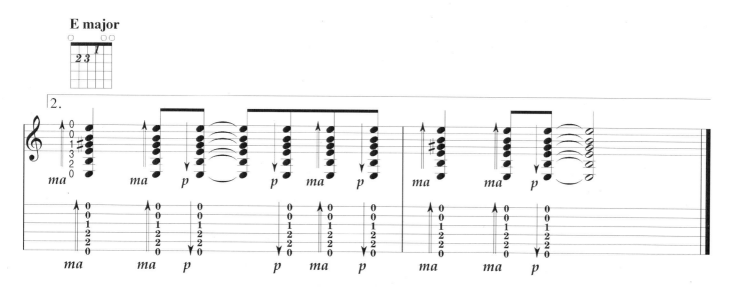

NOTE: The transcription above is a composite of the two versions of this Rumba played in the video, where the first version has four bars on each chord and the second version has two bars. The transcription has two bars on each chord, but the music is repeated, the first time ending on an E7 chord, and the second time on an E major chord. Alternative rhythm patterns B and C shown on page 13 may be played as desired.

Repeats are indicated by dotted bar-lines. The single repeat sign ⎸⁝⎹ tells the player to play again from the beginning.

The indications ⎡1.⎤ ⎡2.⎤ show that the endings are different. Here the last two bars are on E7 the first time and on E major the second time.

Chapter 9   A Modern-Style Rumba Technique

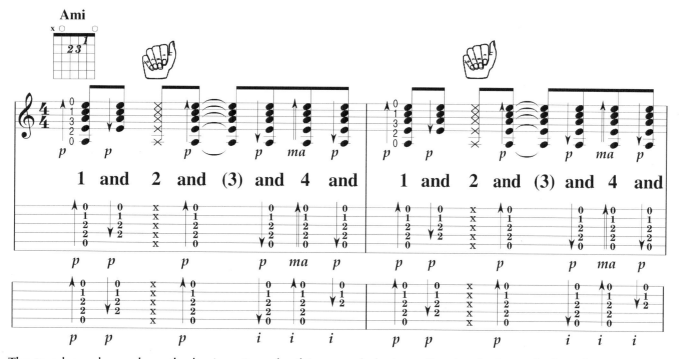

The two bars above show the basic pattern for this way of playing a Rumba rhythm, which is demonstrated in the video through the chord changes Ami, G7, F, E7, Ami, G7, F, E. The notation also shows the counting of the eight half-beats.

The pattern starts with a down-stroke with the thumb, then a thumb up-stroke. Next comes a slap onto the strings with the back of the fingers, shown by the fist symbol above the notation; the notes are shown as 'x's, since the strings do not sound a pitch. The slap is followed by a down-stroke with the thumb on the 4th half-beat (the 'and' after beat 2), and then the three final strokes are as before, up (*p*), down (*ma*), up (*p*) – or, as shown above only in the *cifra*, they can be played with the index finger (*i*), up, down, up. You will see both versions played in the video demonstration. If these final three strokes are played with the index, the last up-stroke may be short, hitting perhaps just the top three strings.

Chapter 10

The Index Finger and Left Hand Apagado

An example of Bulerías in Lebrija style

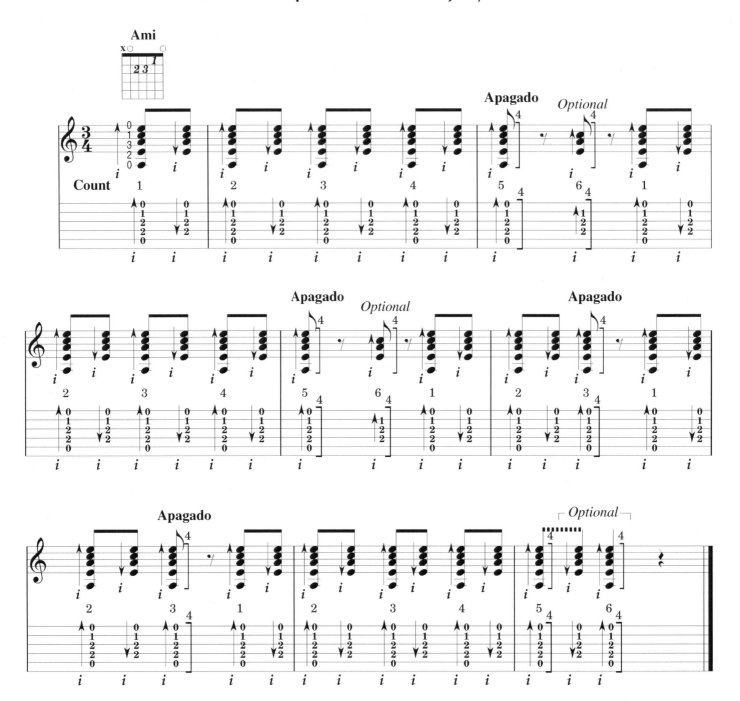

Two *compases* of Bulerías in the Lebrija style are notated above, illustrating the index finger *rasgueo* with down- and up-strokes. The up-strokes tend to be shorter in extent than the down-strokes, striking only the top three or four strings, so they are written to sound just the top four notes.

There are a few minor variations in the repeated video demonstrations of these two *compases*, so some of the strokes and *apagados* are written as 'optional' to encompass these. In the final side-view close-up video, however, these optional strokes are not played, and the *compás* ends with a down-stroke on the count of 5 with an *apagado* immediately following.

A *compás* of Bulerías comprises a pattern of accents within a 12-beat sequence, which may be divided into sections of 6 beats (or 2 times 3 beats), as shown here. The bar-lines in the notation above may be ignored for the present because the counting, as demonstrated in the video, better conveys the feel of the rhythm. They are included, however, in order to be consistent with the way you will see Bulerías discussed and notated when we come to the much more detailed exploration of the *palo* in Volume 2.

The 4-Stroke Rasgueo

The 4-stroke *rasgueo* is written to show each individual stroke of the fingers, with the accent of the *rasgueo* falling on the last stroke, made by the index. It is the index stroke which falls on the beat of the *compas*.

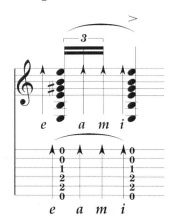

Sometimes, in modern styles of playing, you will see this form of *rasgueo* played with just three-fingers (*a, m, i*) or even just two (*m, i*), but it is important to be able to play the 4-stroke form.

The 4-stroke *rasgueo* is illustrated by its use in the *palo* of Verdiales. In the repeated introductory rhythm section with 3 beats to the bar, you will see that the section ends differently each time it is played. The first time it is played the last bar is on the F chord and the second time there is a descending sequence of chords from G to E. These different endings are indicated by the signs:

1. ⌐   2. ⌐

Verdiales - basic rhythm

Cejilla al dos
Capo at 2nd fret

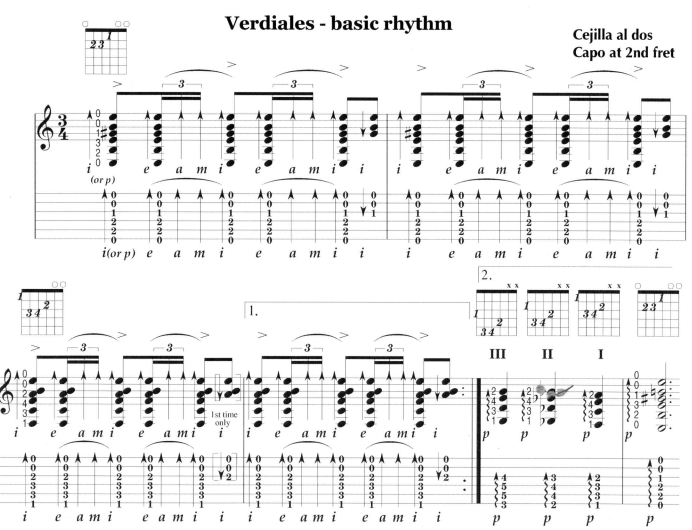

In the first video demonstration of this, all of the above is repeated. The second time through, the initial E chord is replaced by a single note of E on the open 6th string played with the thumb.

Cejilla al dos
Capo at 2nd fret

Chapter 14

Exercise for the thumb (up each string from 6th to 4th, then down)

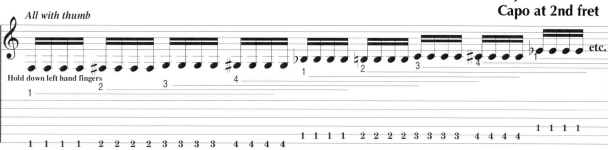

All with thumb

Hold down left hand fingers

VERDIALES FALSETA — illustrating the melodic use of the thumb

The introductory rhythm passage shown on the previous page can be played as an introduction to this first *falseta*. The first bar of the *falseta (below left)* is played instead of the final E chord of the music on the previous page *(below right)*, i.e.

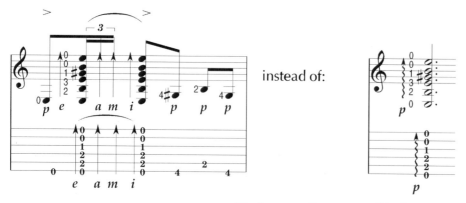

instead of:

Falseta for Verdiales

Note how the left hand fingers that are not stopping the melody notes hold down the chord positions.

Chapter 15

Cejilla al dos
Capo at 2nd fret

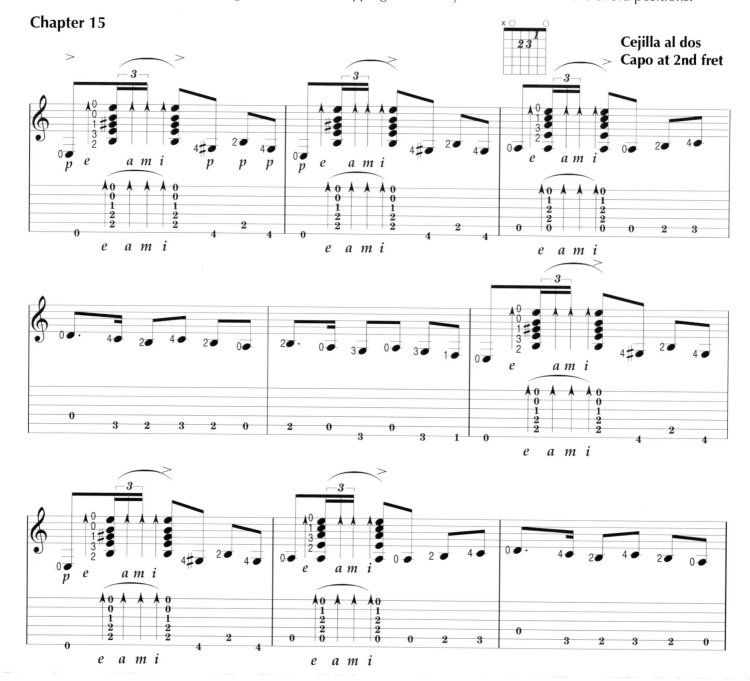

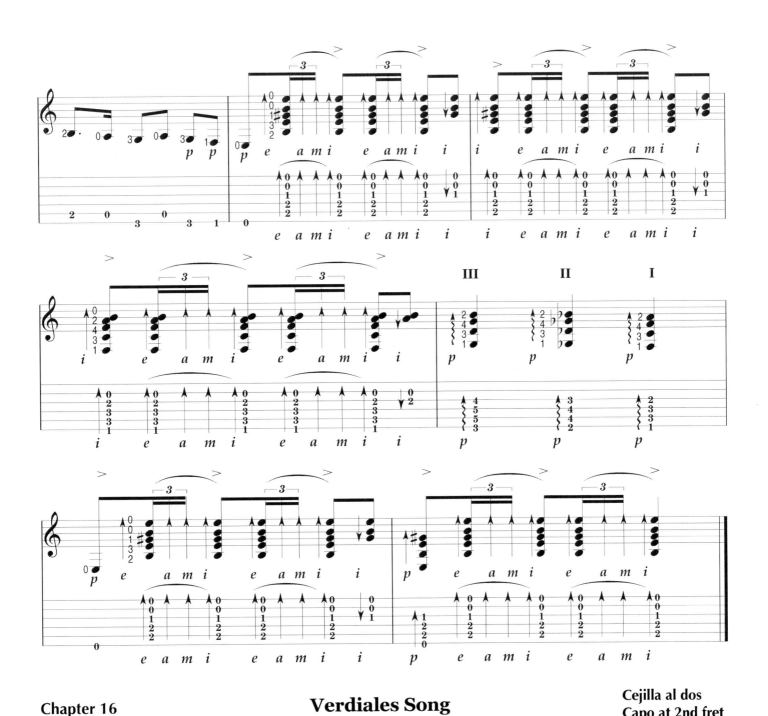

Chapter 16

Verdiales Song

Cejilla al dos
Capo at 2nd fret

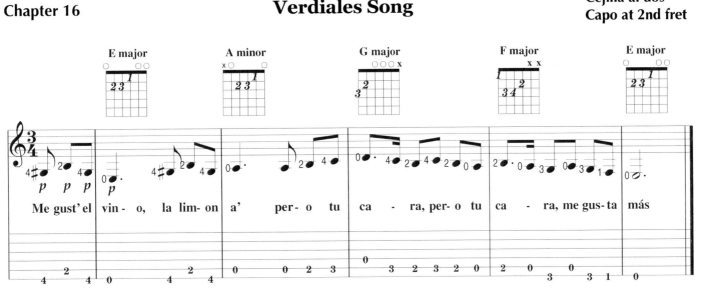

Me gust'el vin - o, la lim-on a' per-o tu ca - ra, per-o tu ca - ra, me gus-ta más

Chapter 17

Chords in the *por medio* Position

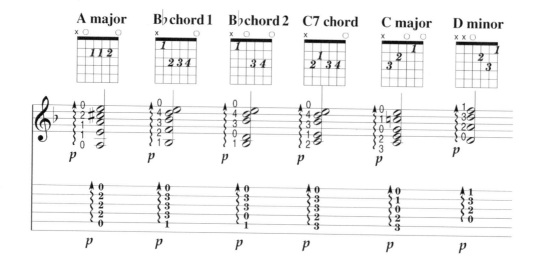

In the *por medio* position the root chord is A major, and the flamenco Phrygian sequence is based around D minor, C (or C7, here with an added 9th note, D), B flat and A. This corresponds to the sequence we saw earlier of A minor, G (or G7) F, E in the *por arriba* position. It's called 'Phrygian' because of the similarity of this characteristically flamenco sequence to the Phrygian mode or scale.

In the following brief illustration of the rhythm of Tientos, we see flamenco variations of the B flat chords, which are here named B flat chords 1 and 2. The second chord of the piece is not named, as it is a transitional chord played as the left hand fingers move from the A major chord to a B flat 1 chord.

In the video demonstration of the left hand positions for the chords the B flat 2 chord is shown but not the B flat 1, which has the second finger stopping the 4th string at the 3rd fret (F). Both of these forms of a flamenco B flat chord are played in the video excerpt of Tientos.

The pitches of the chords are named as if the *cejilla* was not used. When it is used, we should more strictly speak of the chords as being in the A shape, the C shape etc.

Chapter 18   **Tientos Chords and Rhythm**   **Cejilla al tres**
Capo at 3rd fret

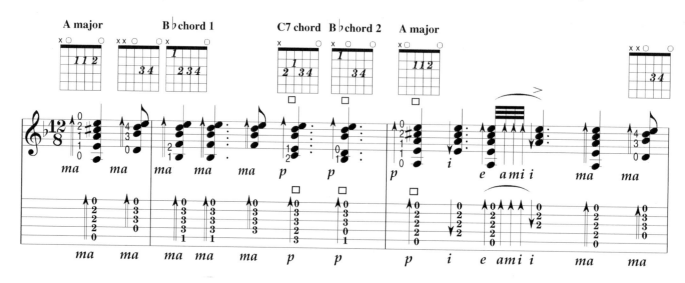

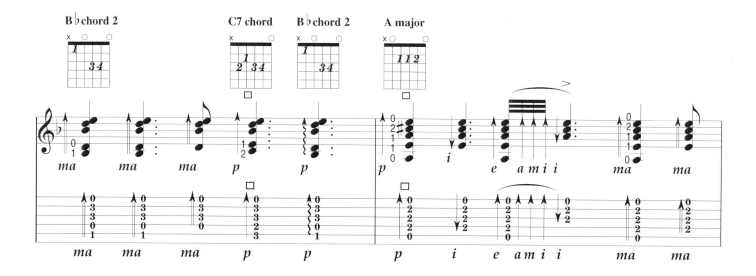

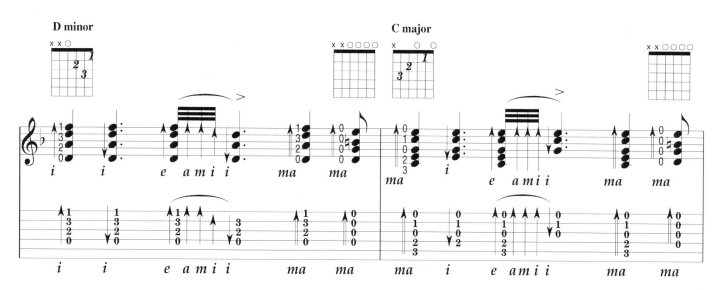

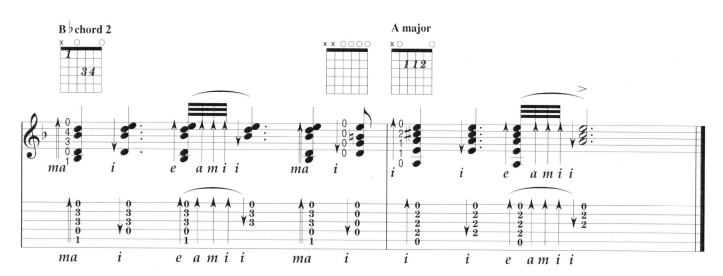

NOTE: In the above demonstration of chords in the *por medio* position, 5-stroke *rasgueos* are shown, as played in the video. This technique, in which the accent here falls on a fifth stroke, an up-stroke with the index after a 4-stroke *rasgueo*, is demonstrated later in the video at Chapter 39. 4-stroke *rasgueos*, with the accent on the final stroke by the index finger, may be played instead. There are also *golpes* combined with a thumb down-stroke in the first 4 bars. These may be ignored for the moment: the technique is demonstrated at Chapter 41.

Chapter 19

First Tientos

Cejilla al dos
Capo at 2nd fret

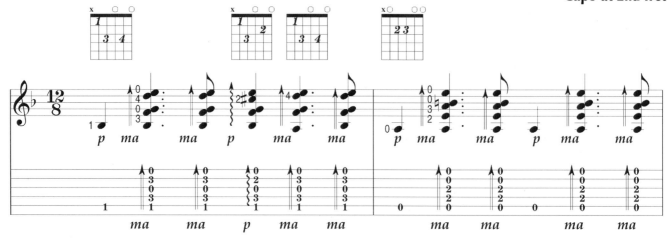

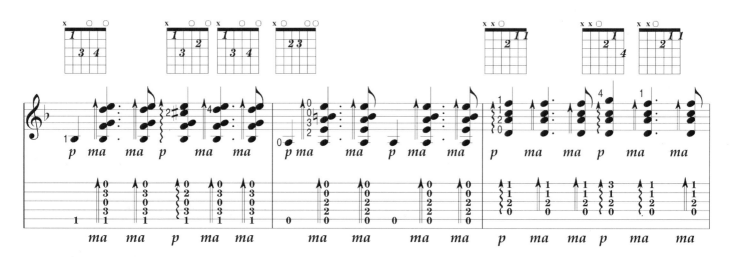

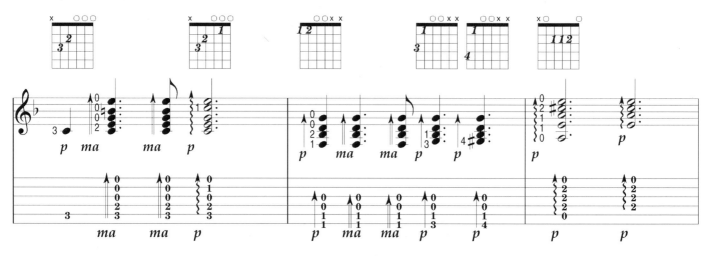

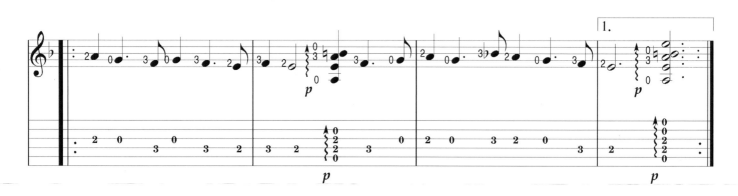

Chapter 20   **Ligado Exercise** (on all six strings)

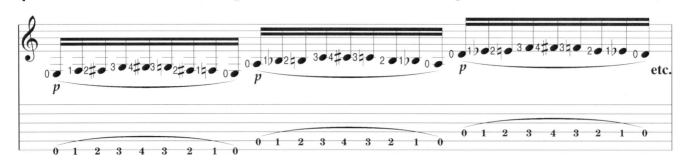

Chapter 21   **Falseta for Alegrías *por rosas***

Cejilla al dos
Capo at 2nd fret

* Notes marked with an asterisk are played the first time the *falseta* is demonstrated, but are omitted in the second slower version. They are optional.

4-Stroke Rasgueo in Tangos (with *golpes*)

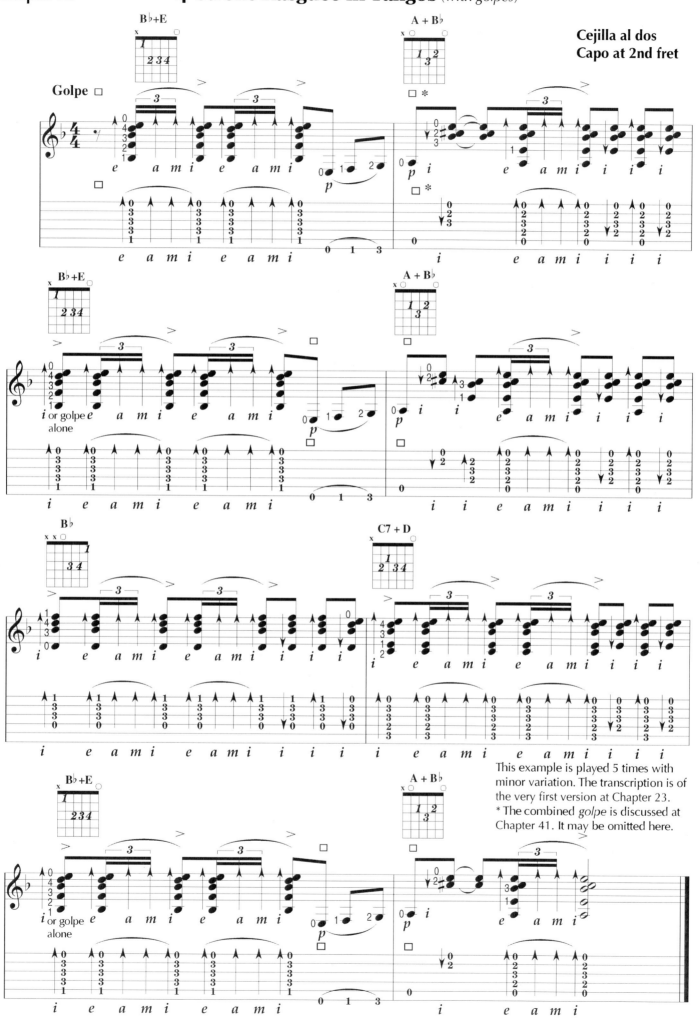

Cejilla al dos
Capo at 2nd fret

This example is played 5 times with minor variation. The transcription is of the very first version at Chapter 23.
* The combined *golpe* is discussed at Chapter 41. It may be omitted here.

Tangos 2: *por arriba* (with song 'El agua se va pa' los ríos')

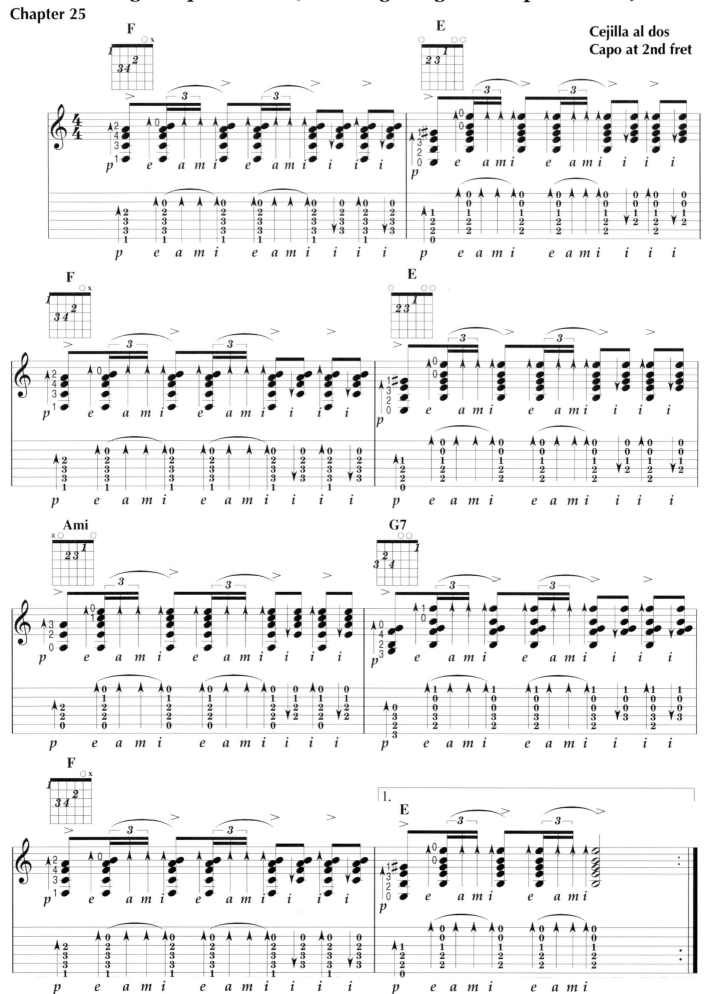

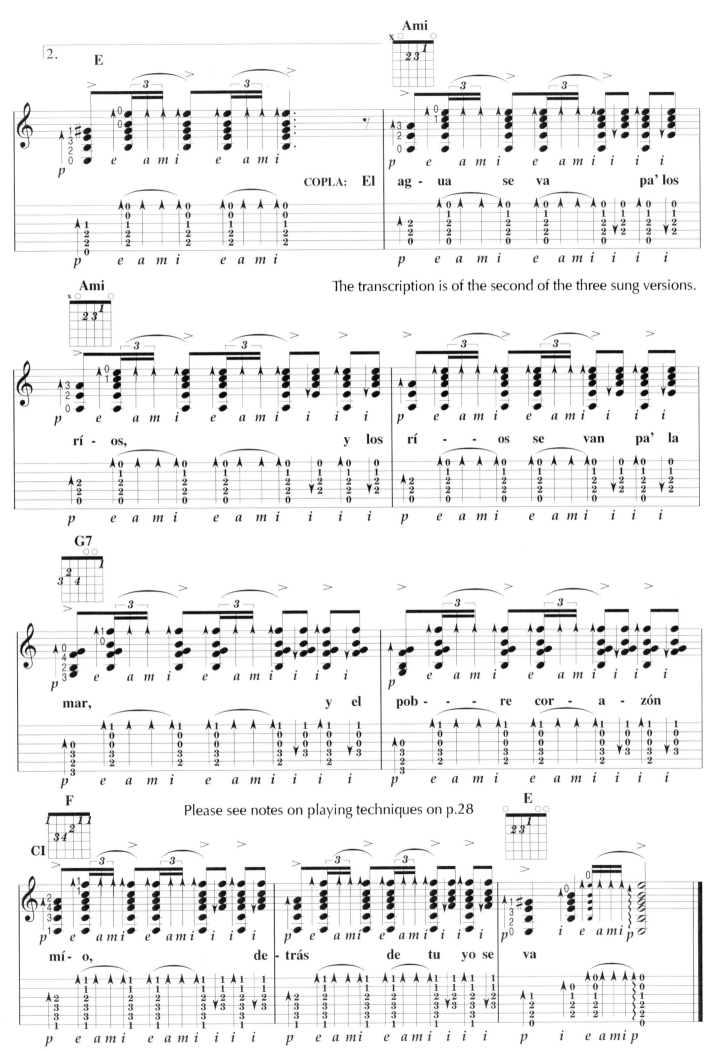

The transcription is of the second of the three sung versions.

Please see notes on playing techniques on p.28

NOTE: In the final line of music on the previous page, p.27, two techniques are shown which are demonstrated later in the video: (1) A full 6-string chord of F major is used with a first finger *barré* across all 6 strings. (2) The final chord is played as a thumb-stroke preceded by a fast 4-stroke *rasgueo*. These are demonstrated later in the video, at Chapter 26 and Chapter 51 (and notated on page 48), respectively.

Song Tune *(picado)*

NOTE: The rule that index and middle fingers should always alternate in *picado* playing applies when playing at a fast tempo. It need not always apply when playing a slow passage such as the above. The transcription above is of the second time it is played.

A flamenco vibrato technique is here shown on the held A and F notes, the left hand finger rapidly pulling and relaxing the string, at right-angles to the fretboard.

Chapters 27, 29, 31 & 34

Picado Exercises

Picado Exercise 1. on all strings from 1 to 6 then 6 to 1. In the first demonstration of this exercise at Chapter 27, eight notes are played on each string..

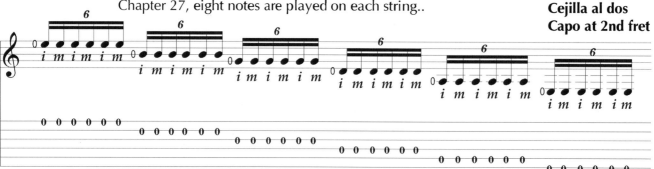

Picado Exercise 2.

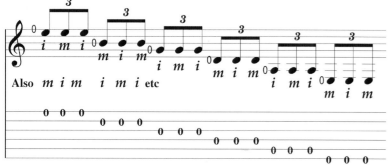

Picado Exercise 3.

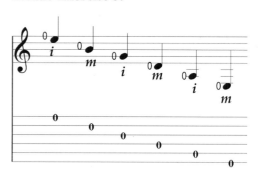

Picado Exercise 4.

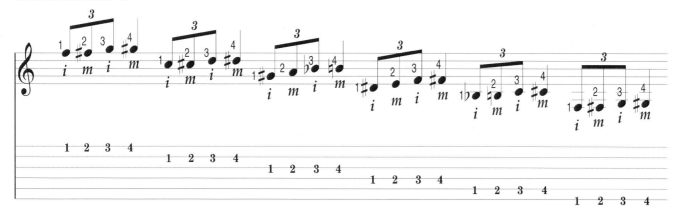

Picado Exercise 5.

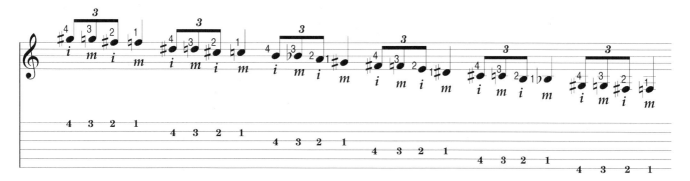

The following *picado* exercises are demonstrated at **Chapter 34**, later in the video than the previous three, but are written here for ease of reference when *picado* is practiced.

Picado Exercise 6.

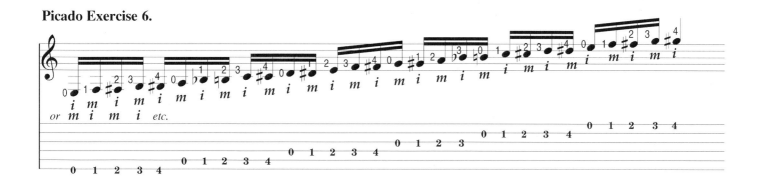

Picado Exercise 7.

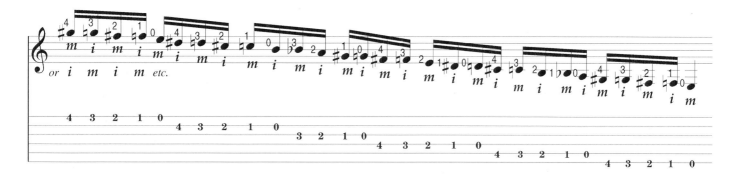

NOTE: In the final two staves of music on the following page, p.31, and also in the next *falseta* on p.33, 5-stroke *rasgueos* are shown, as demonstrated in the video. This technique, in which the accent falls on a fifth stroke, an up-stroke with the index, is also demonstrated later in the video at menu item Chapter 39. 4-stroke *rasgueos*, with the accent on the final down-stroke by the index finger, may be played instead.

Chapter 30   Zapateado *Falseta*

The transcription is of the first, faster version played in the video. The second and third versions have a G added at the 3rd fret of the first string for the chords of C7 (now C) and C in the 3rd line of music on p.31, as demonstrated in the video.

Cejilla al dos
Capo at 2nd fret

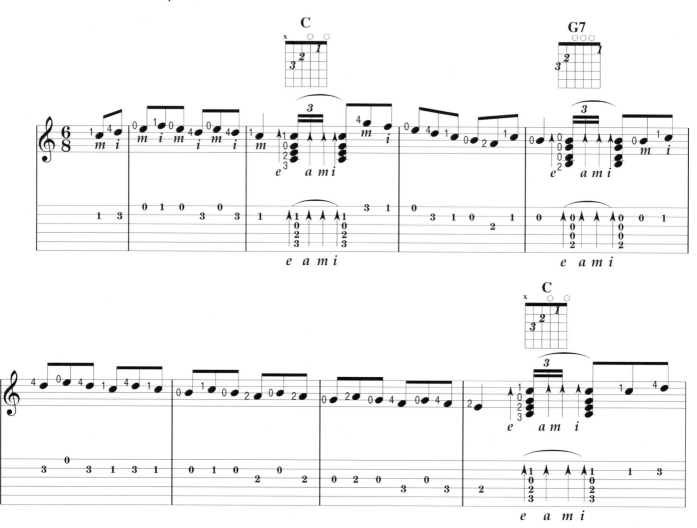

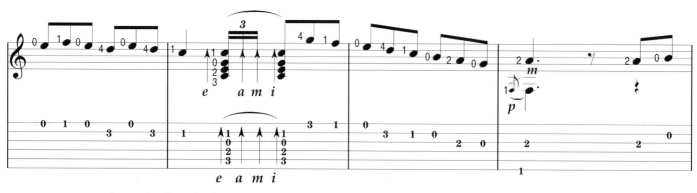

A grace note is shown before the bass note F (on the 6th string) in the final bar on this page. This indicates that the bass note played by the thumb is sounded slightly before the higher note (here A, played by the second finger on the 3rd string), as also indicated in the tab. This technique will be seen often in the pages following, for example in the Farruca excerpt on pages 44 and 45.

Another Zapateado Falseta

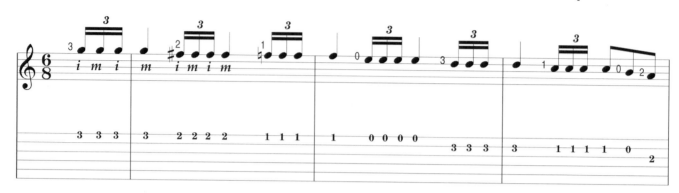

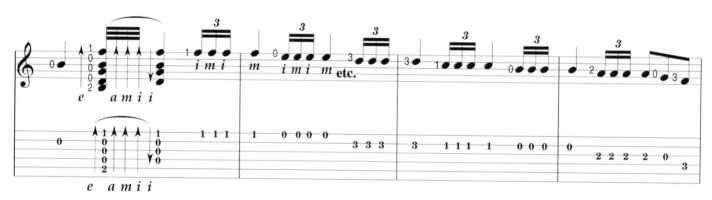

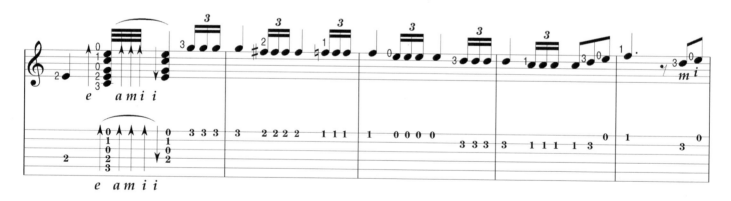

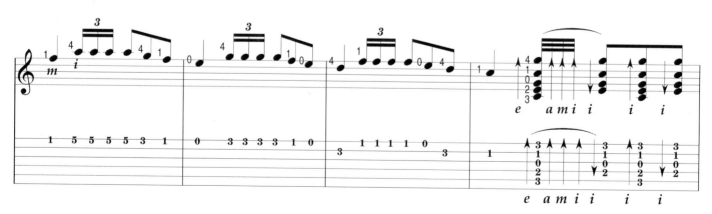

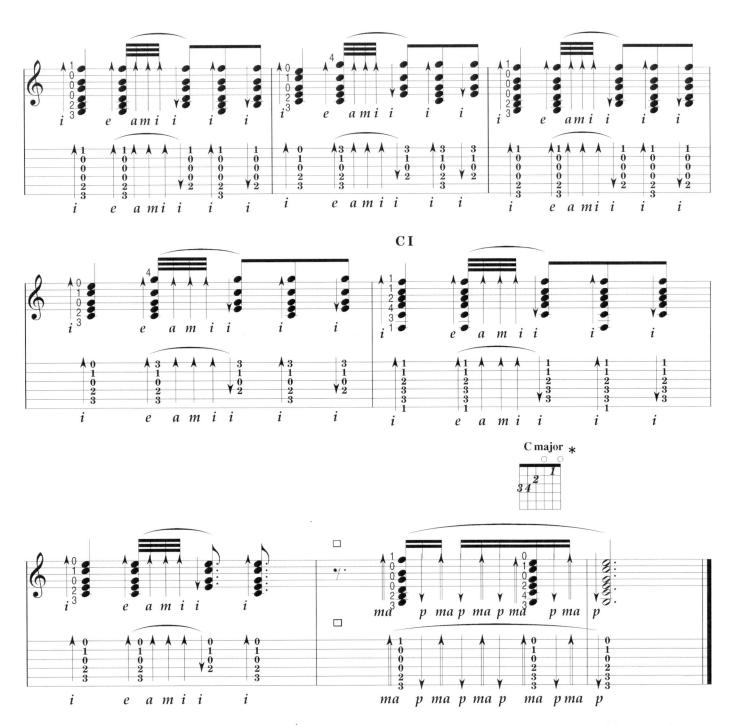

Chapter 32

* When this ending is demonstrated at a slow speed the chord change to C is not made until the final up-stroke with the thumb.

The triplet *rasgueo* shown above in the penultimate bar is a different technique from the triplet *rasgueos* demonstrated later. These will be written (see page 47) as follows:

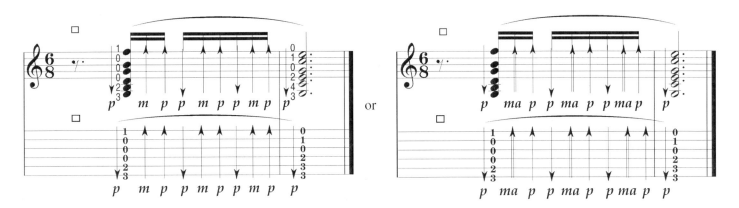

Ligado 'hammering on' and 'pulling off' are first demonstrated in relation to the Taranta, a free form *palo* *(toque libre)* which does not have a regular beat. Closely related in its chordal structure is the Taranto, a strongly rhythmic *palo*. The *arrastre* is particularly used in the Taranta in both its partial and complete forms written out below.

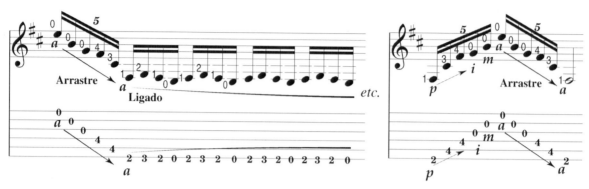

Chapter 38   Taranto

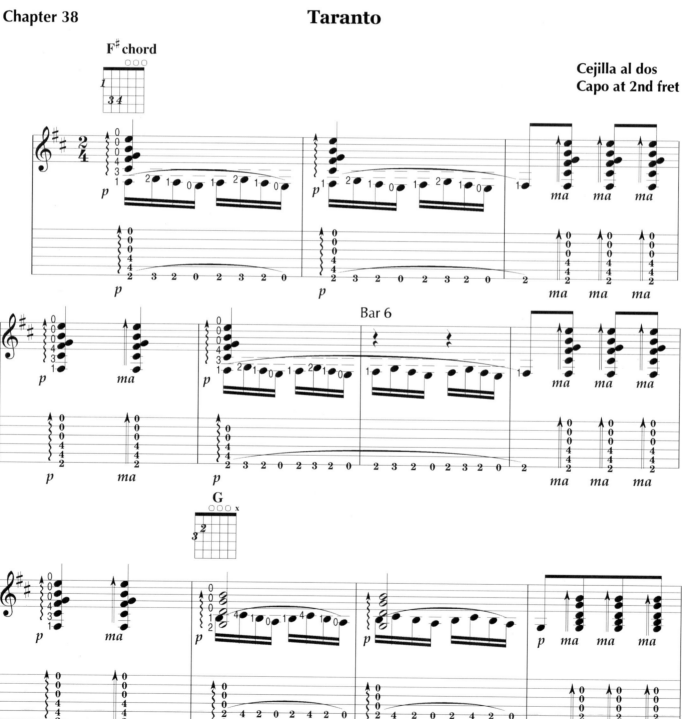

The transcription above is of the first version demonstrated in the video. In the second version bar 6 is the same as bar 5, the A note is repeated in bar 20 in the same rhythm as bar 22 and the repeated G note in the 3rd bar from the end (after the dotted G) is omitted.

Comparing the 5-, 4- and 3-stroke Rasgueos

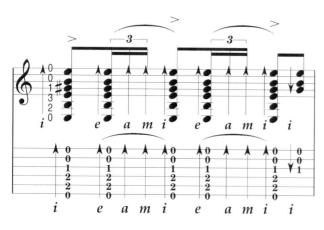

In the standard 4-stroke *rasgueo* (left, from Verdiales), the beat falls on the fourth down-stroke, with the index. In the 5-stroke *rasgueo (below)*, the beat may fall on the fifth stroke, the index up-stroke, as previously in Zapateado, or it may fall on the first down-stroke, with the little finger as here in Soleá. Similarly, in the double 5-stroke *rasgueo*, the beats fall on the initial strokes with the little finger. In the 4-stroke *rasgueo* played with *a, m, i, i* (omitting the little finger), demonstrated in the video with the fingers flicking out against the thumb to give a staccato feel, the beat falls on the third finger, *a*. These *rasgueos* are shown below, each in one 12-beat *compás* of the Soleá.

The 5-stroke *rasgueo* in Soleá

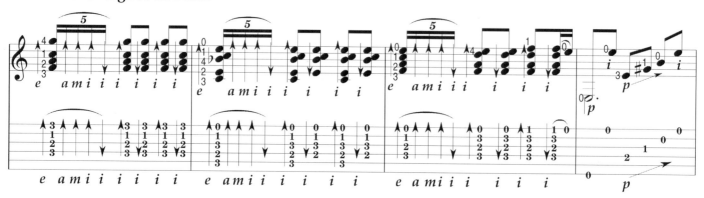

The double 5-stroke *rasgueo*

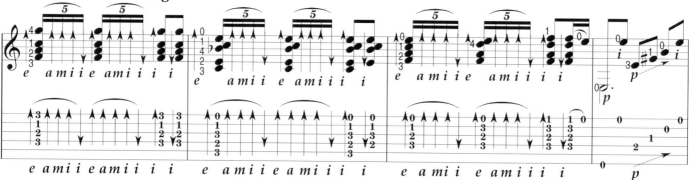

4-stroke *rasgueo* with *a, m, i, i* (3-stroke *rasgueo* plus index up-stroke)

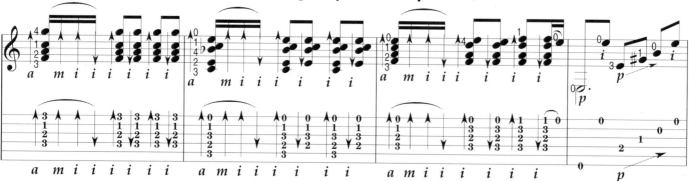

The above *compás* is demonstrated in the video with or without a G at the third fret of the first string in the first bar and a C major or C7 chord in the second bar.

The 5-stroke *rasgueo* is again demonstrated in the rhythmic introduction to a Soleá transcribed on the next page. Each line of music contains one 12-beat *compás* of the rhythm. The *palo* of Soleá receives more detailed coverage in a later section of this volume. Each *compás* is written here in the conventional way as four bars of three beats each, but the accents of the rhythm fall on beats 3, 6, 8, 10 and 12. Ending beats fall on beat 10.

Introduction to the Soleá

illustrating the basic *compás* and the 5-stroke *rasgueo*

Cejilla al dos
Capo at 2nd fret

See p. 48

Arpegios: illustrated by the Escobilla of Alegrías

Cejilla al dos
Capo at 2nd fret

1. Thumb and index (*p,i*)

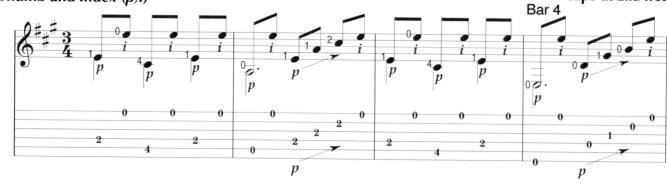
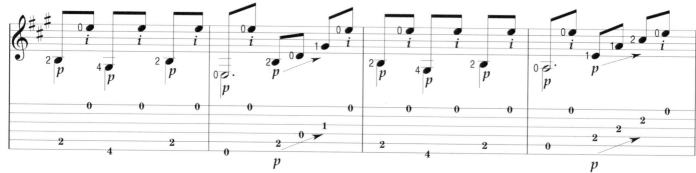

The music above shows the slower version. When this passage is played faster, bar 4 *(left)* is replaced by one of the bars on the right because the thumb cannot easily jump over the fifth string at speed. At the fastest speed all the bars may be played just with alternating thumb and index strokes, as on the far right.

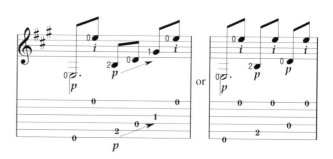

Chapter 43

2. Thumb, index, middle fingers (*p,i,m*)

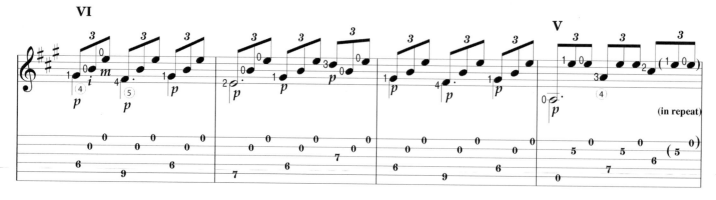

Chapter 44

3. Thumb, ring, middle, index fingers (*p,a,m,i*) – 'Back' *Arpegio* – *Arpegio sencillo* (and *p,i,m,a*)

4. Fast 'Forward' *Arpegio* (*p,i,m,a*) – the transcription is of the first, longer version demonstrated.

5. *Escobilla* tune with fast forward *i,m,a* Arpegios

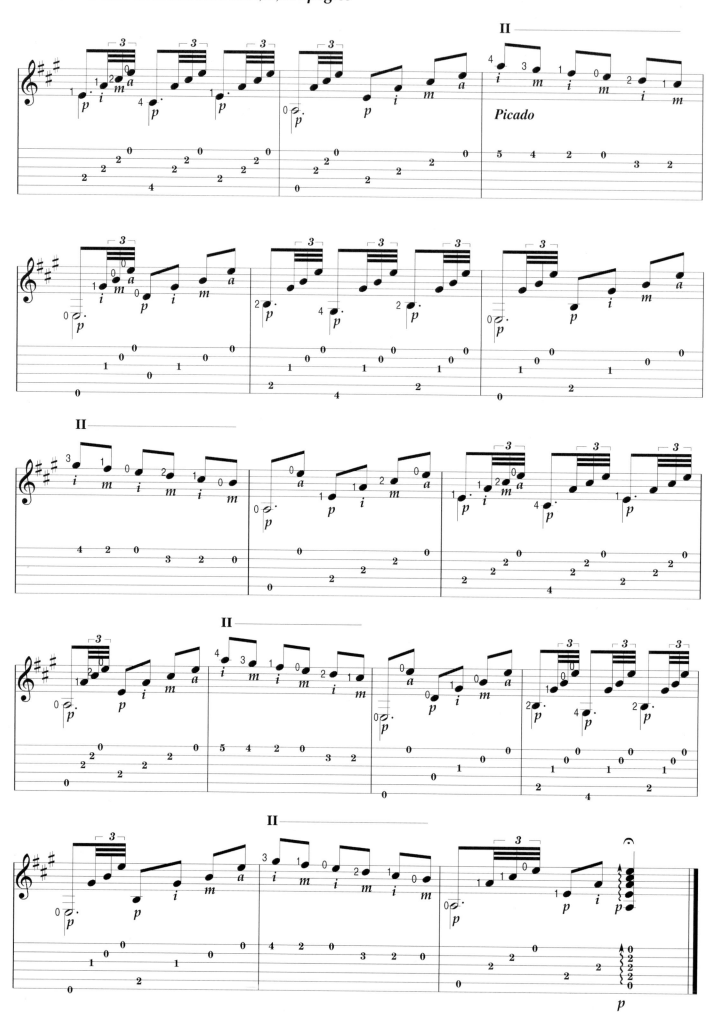

Chapter 45

6. *Campanela Arpegio*

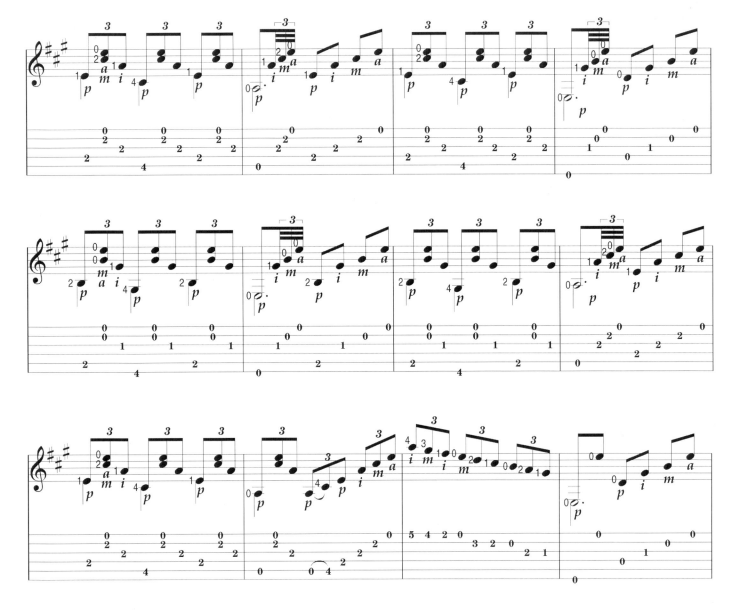

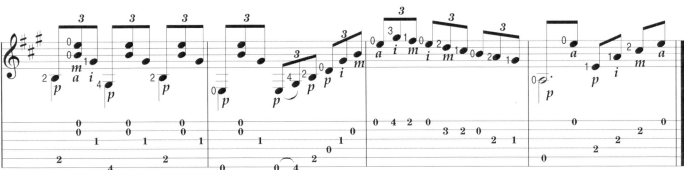

Campanela Technique in Zapateado

Cejilla al dos
Capo at 2nd fret

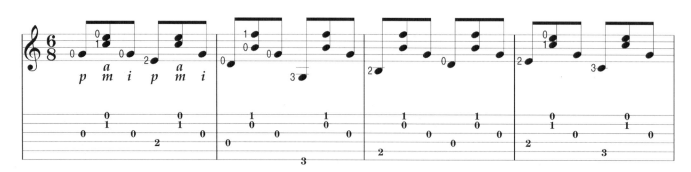

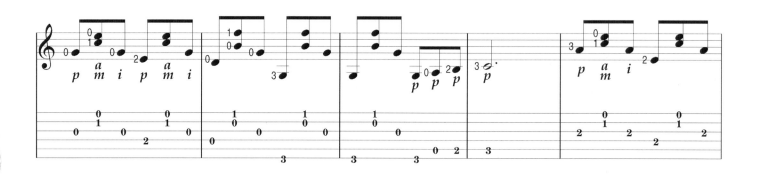

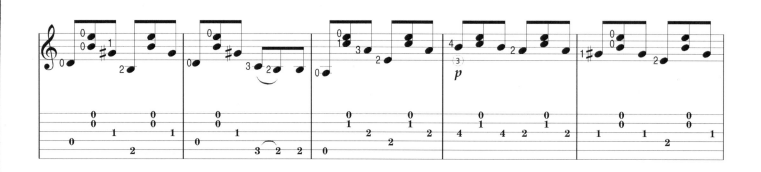

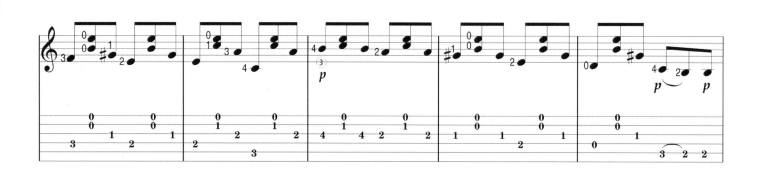

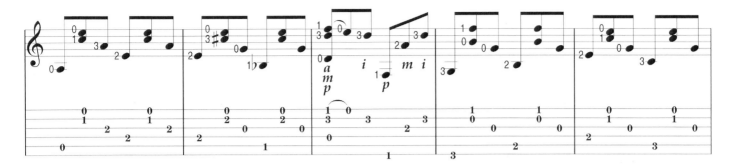

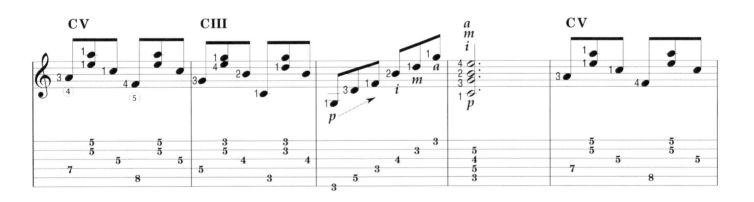

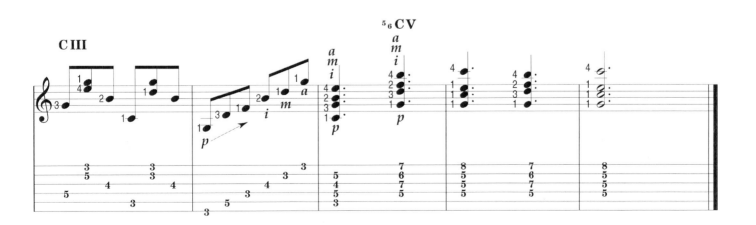

Back and Forward Arpegios in Farruca

Back arpegio *p,a,m,i*

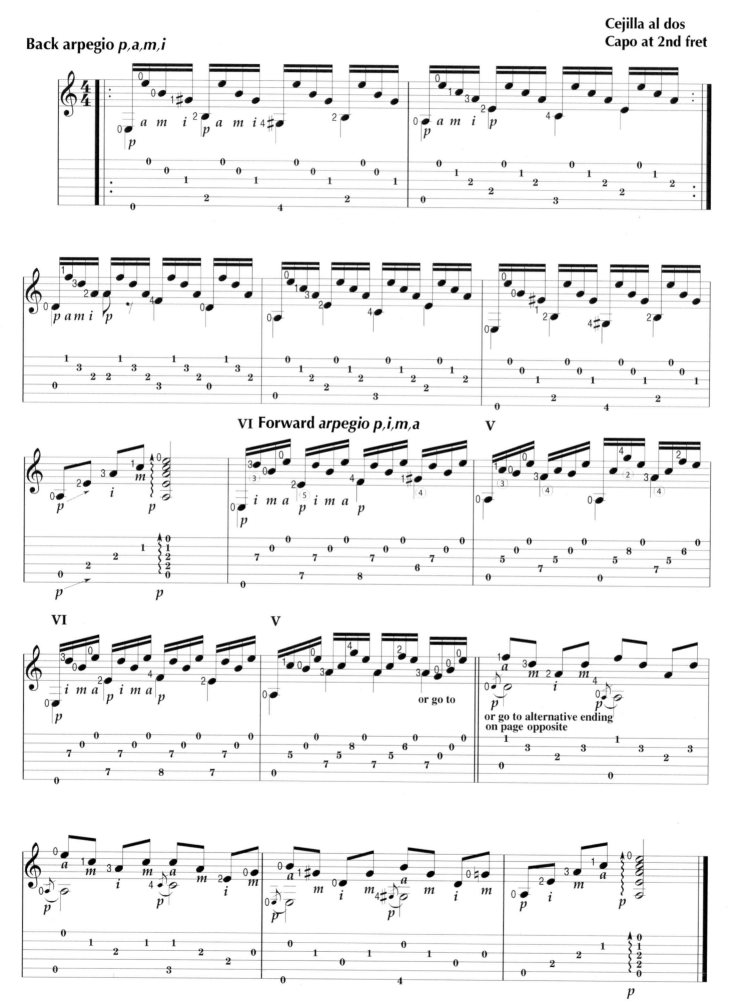

VI Forward *arpegio p,i,m,a*   **V**

or go to

or go to alternative ending
on page opposite

An Alternative Ending for Farruca

A grace note is shown before bass notes in the final four bars of the Farruca on the previous page, and others are shown before the D and A in the above alternative ending. As previously mentioned on page 30, these indicate that the bass notes played by the thumb are played slightly before the higher note (here played by the third finger), as also indicated in the tab.

Juan's company performing in Istanbul. Miguel Infante is dancing.

Chapter 48

'Continual' Rasgueo and Alzapúa

an example of Seguiriyas

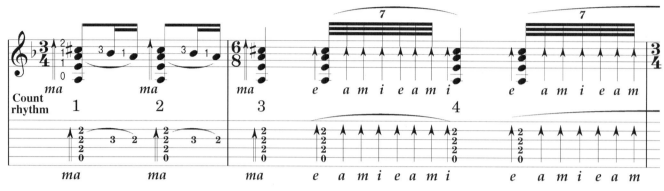

Four-stroke rasgueo repeated six times

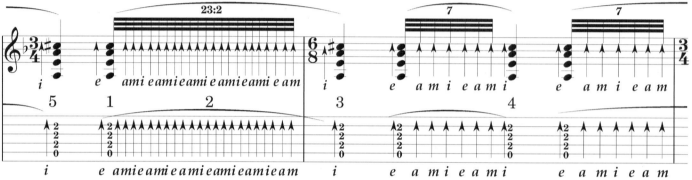

Four-stroke rasgueo repeated six times

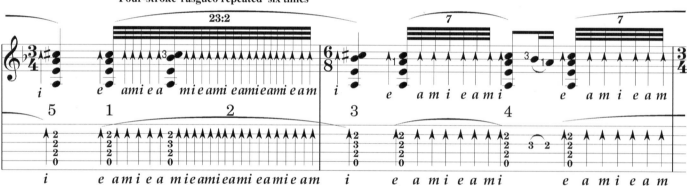

see page 48

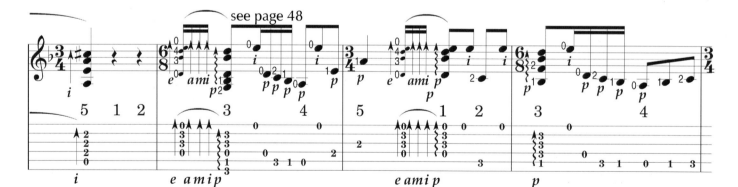

Alzapúa

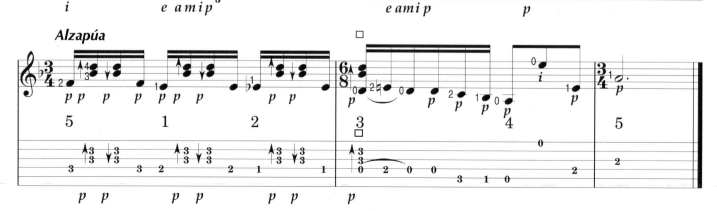

Alzapúa Exercise

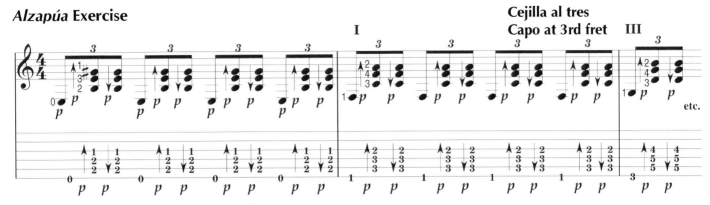

Triplet *rasgueos*

Chapter 50

Either of these, for example, could be an ending for Zapateado, as previously mentioned on page 33.

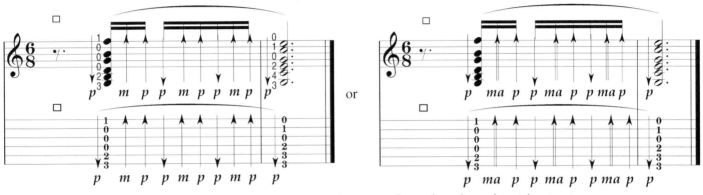

or

The following two 12-beat *compases* of Alegrías are shown in the video (from the side view):

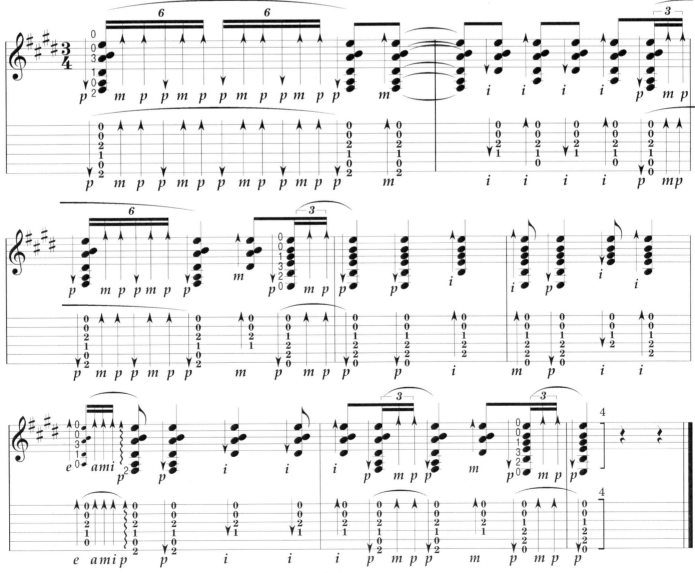

47

Rasgueo followed by the thumb (A technique of Niño Ricardo)

Chapter 51

'from the side angle'

Chapter 52

Flamenco Trémolo

The 5-note *trémolo* is used for melodic playing, imitating a solo instrument with bass accompaniment. A bass note played by the thumb is followed by four *tirando* finger strokes, *i,a,m,i*, within the duration of one beat.

This *(right)* shows the *trémolo* thumb-stroke, with *i,a,m,i* before the thumb plays across the strings. In faster rhythms just the three fingers, *a,m,i*, may be played, as shown later.

The *trémolo* thumb-stroke in a *compás* of Soleá

Exercises for Trémolo

An exercise on one string:

Sin cejilla
Without capo

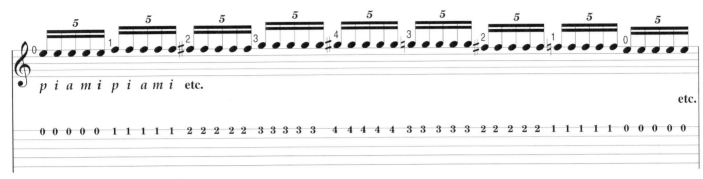

p i a m i p i a m i etc.

Repeat similarly on the 2nd string.

Trémolo Falseta

The melodic *trémolo* in a *falseta* for Farruca

Sin cejilla
Without capo

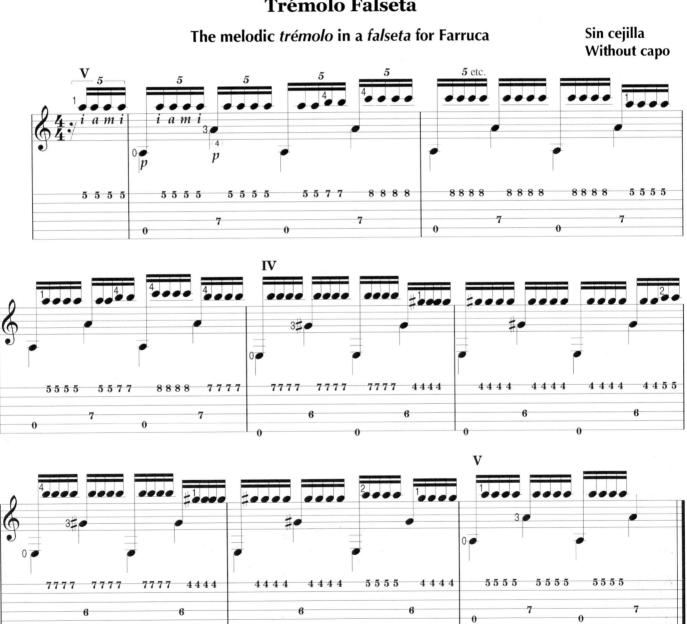

In flamenco *trémolo* the four melody notes of each group are not always the same, as is seen above. The player has the freedom to impart his or her own interpretation of the melody, giving it a personal feel and flow. This reflects the fact that flamenco is an improvised music based on an aural tradition rather than a written score. For this reason transcription of a passage of *trémolo* may be somewhat approximate if it is not to become excessively difficult to follow exactly.

Fandango *por medio*

The transcription is of the first, slower version at Chapter 54.

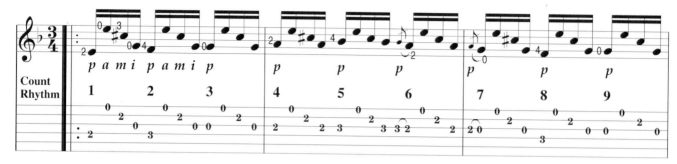

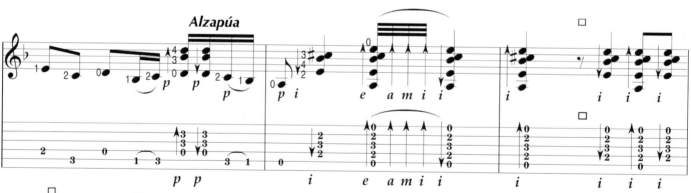

Soleá

The basic *compás* of the Soleá, its recurring rhythmic element, consists of twelve beats, accented on beats 3, 6, 8, 10 and 12. Endings may occur on beat 10.

The twelve beats are commonly, as here, written as four bars of three beats each, in 3/4 time. The accents of the *compás* do not fall on the first beat of each bar. Other methods of notation have sometimes been used, but offer no clear advantages since they tend to be more complicated.

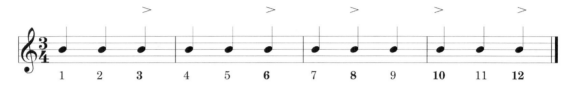

Chapter 56
The excerpt of the dance and singing that introduces this section starts with a *falseta*, transcribed on the following page.

Carlos Brias sings por Soleá. Raquel de Luna dances.

Opening Falseta for Dance Introduction to Soleá

Chapter 56

Cejilla al seis
Capo at 6th fret

Juan's cross-cultural group, Música Alhambra.

The Compás of Soleá (Two 12-beat *compases*)

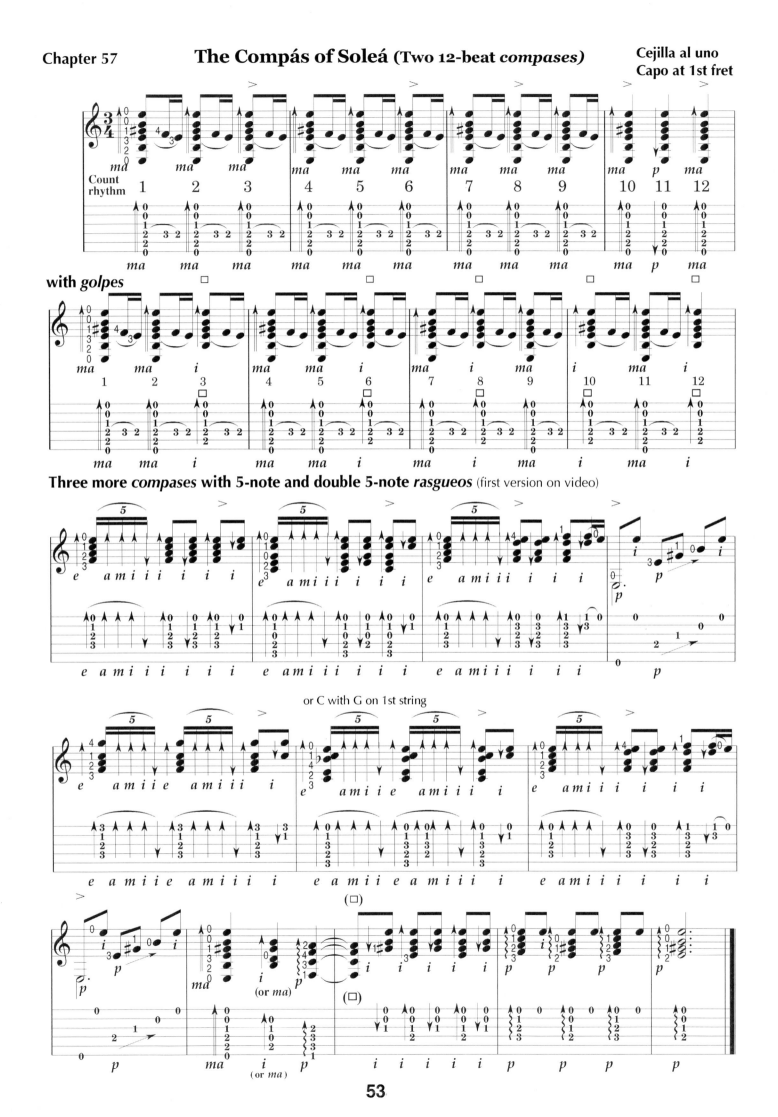

with *golpes*

Three more *compases* with 5-note and double 5-note *rasgueos* (first version on video)

or C with G on 1st string

Chapter 58   With doubled beats

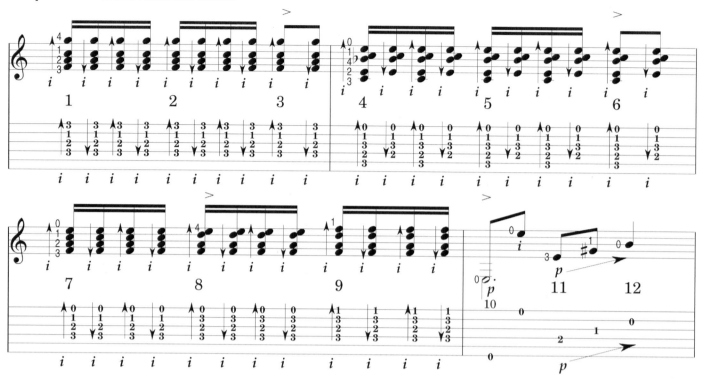

The video demonstrations of these preceding and following *compases* show minor variations. The chord for the first 3 beats may optionally have the 1st string stopped at the 3rd fret (G) or left open. The chord for the second 3 beats may be of C major (with or without G at the 3rd fret on the first string) or C7 with B flat at the 3rd fret on the 3rd string. When the *compases* are first played as if for the dancer 'El Tigre', there is an *apagado* with the left little finger after the 3rd and 6th beats, as shown below:

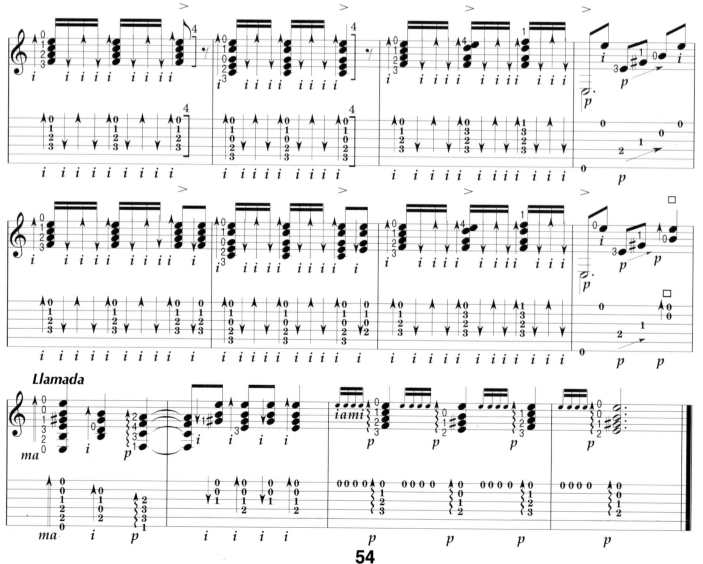

Chapter 59

Chords for Soleá de Alcalá

The transcription is of the first version demonstrated.

continued overleaf

Alternative ending – *cierre*

Adding Interest: More Soleá Ritmeo

The transcription is of the first version demonstrated.

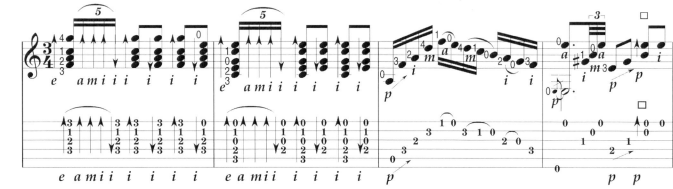
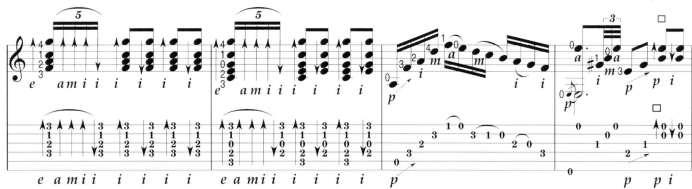
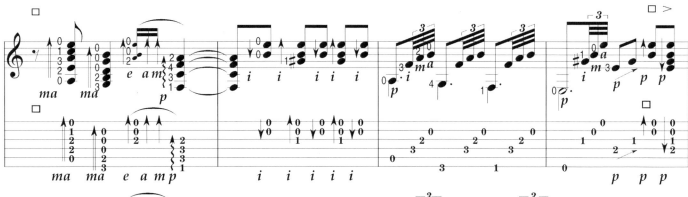
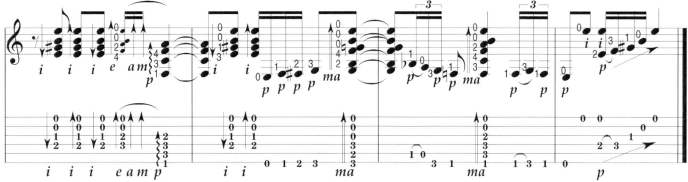

Alternative endings

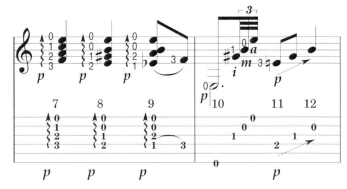
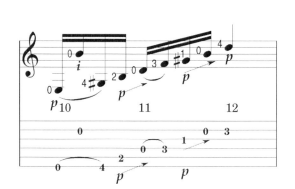

Soleá: Adding Syncopation

The first three staves of music contain two 12-beat *compases*, counted as shown. All other staves contain one *compás* in each.

Cejilla al uno
Capo at 1st fret

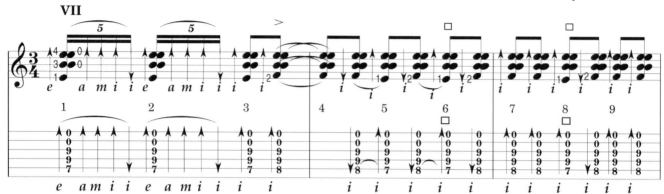

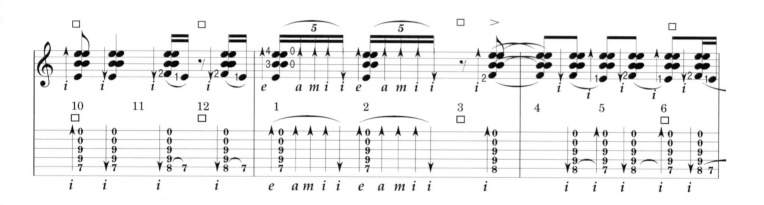

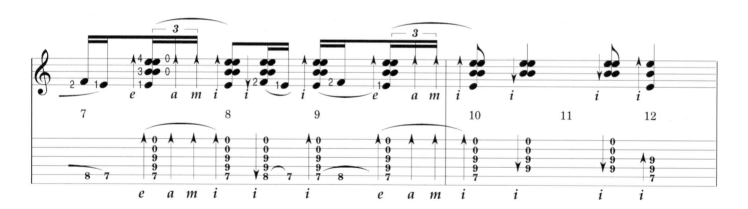

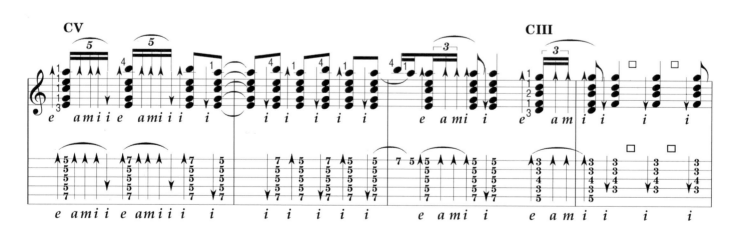

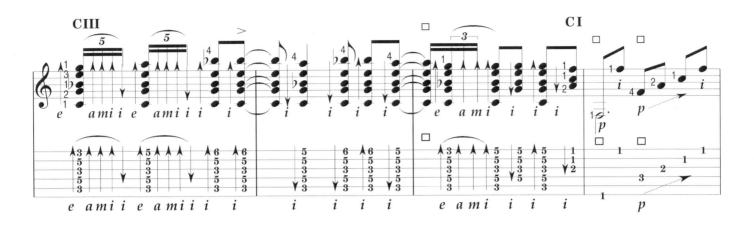

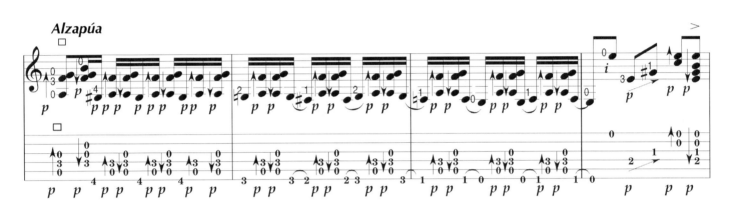

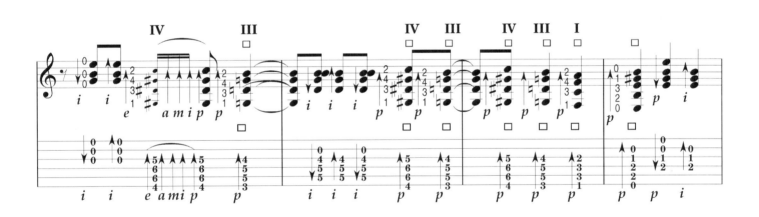

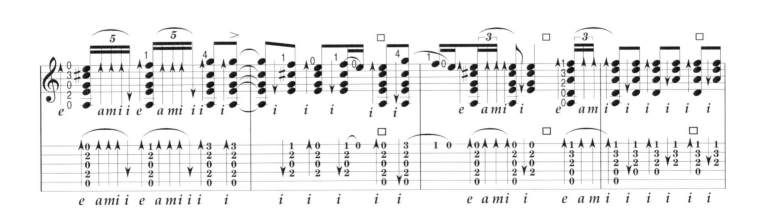

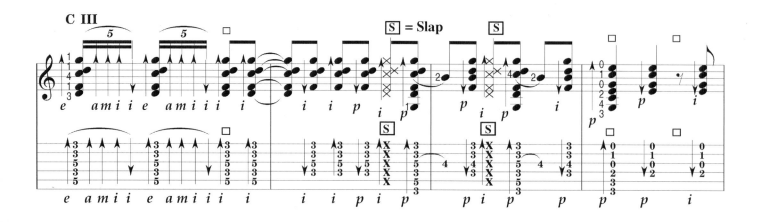

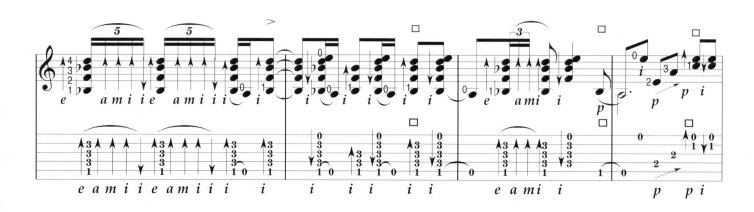

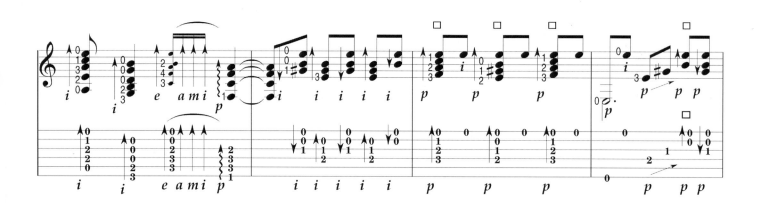

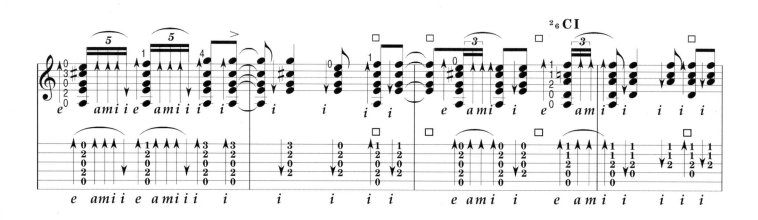

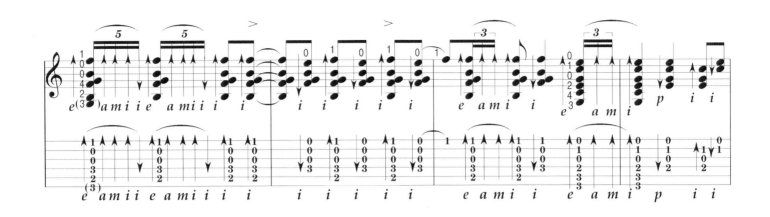

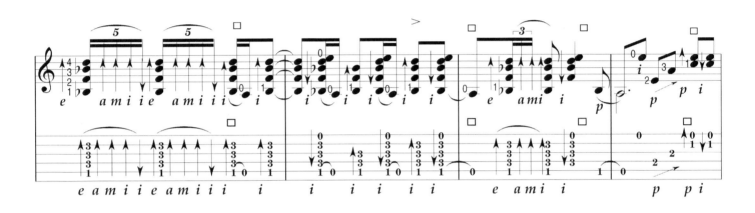

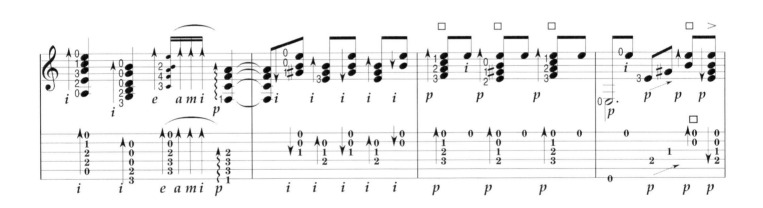

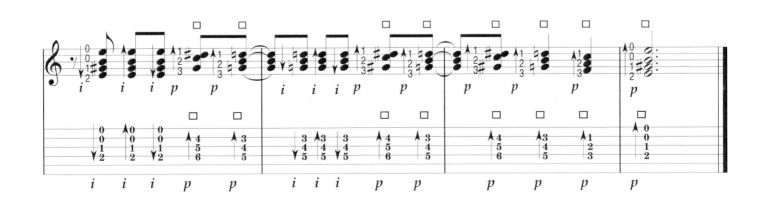

Chapter 62

Soleá: Simpler Ritmeo

Cejilla al uno
Capo at 1st fret

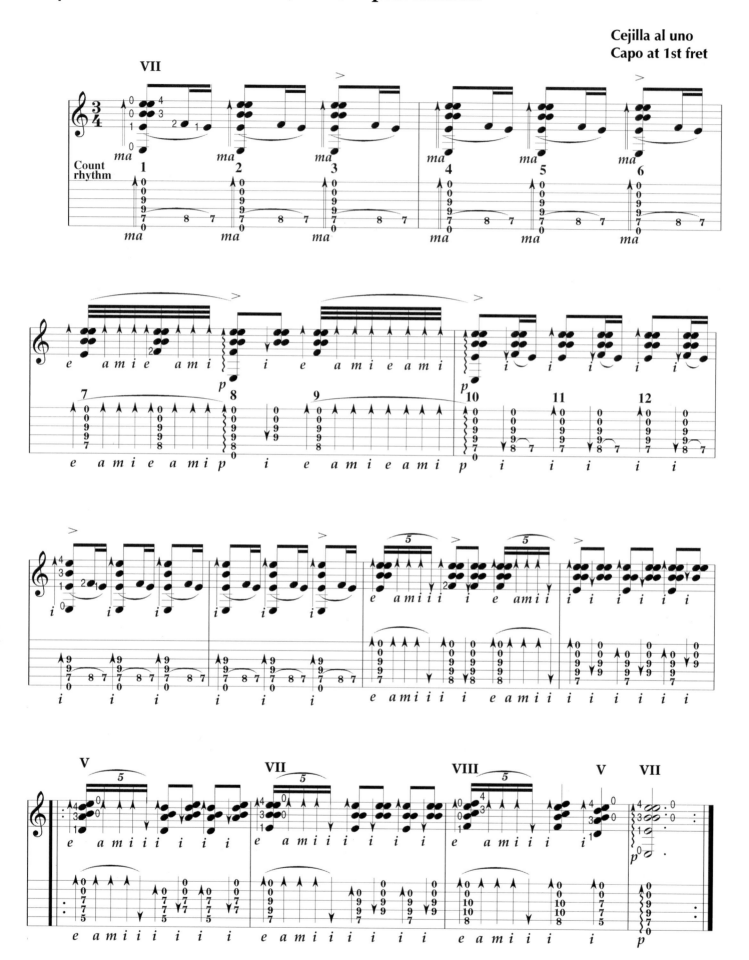

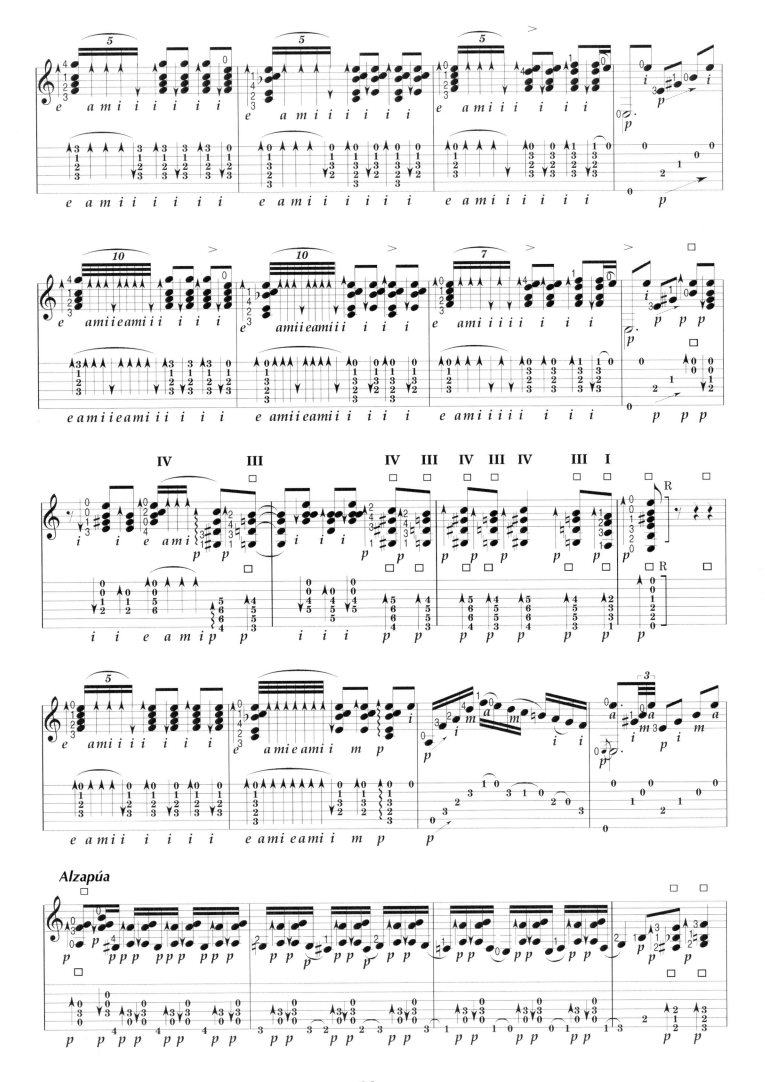

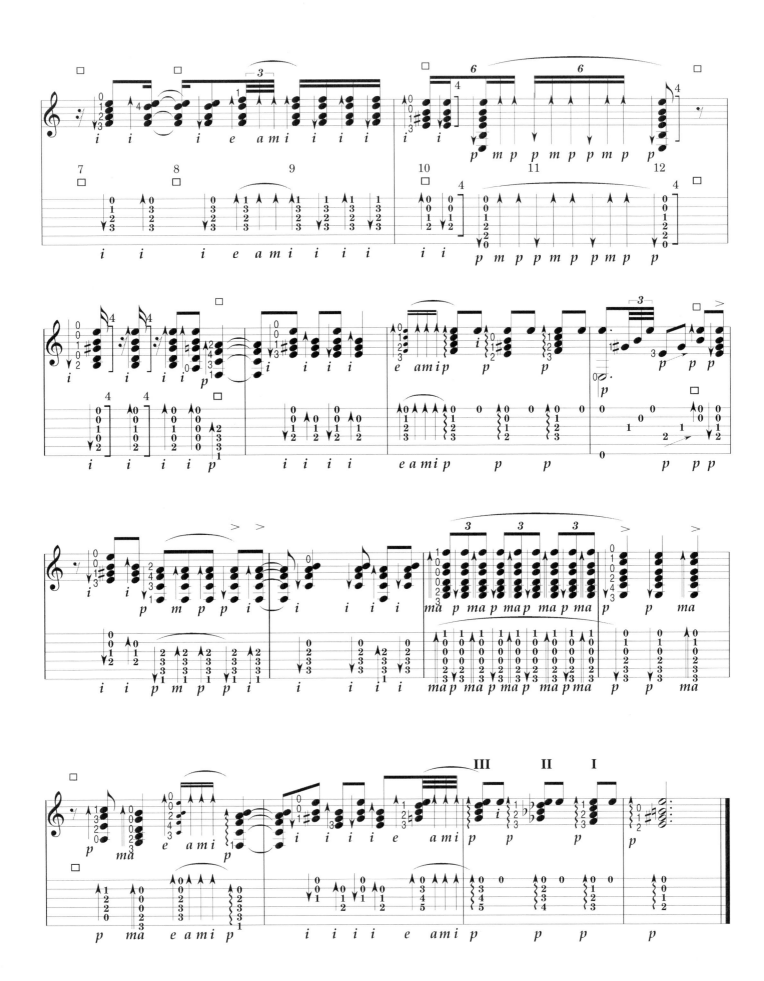

The sequence 'Alzapúa and Ritmeo' on the video (at Chapter 63) is not transcribed. It is a further demonstration of compases included among the above.

Chapter 64

Transition to Falsetas

Cejilla al cuatro
Capo at 4th fret

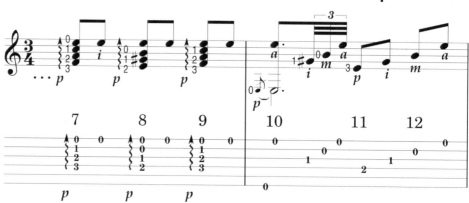

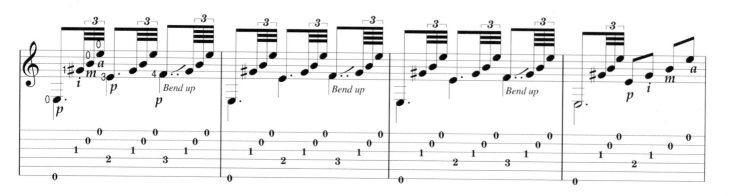

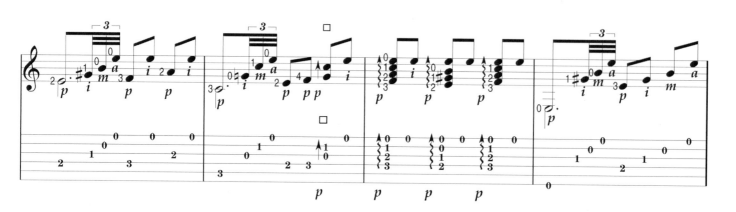

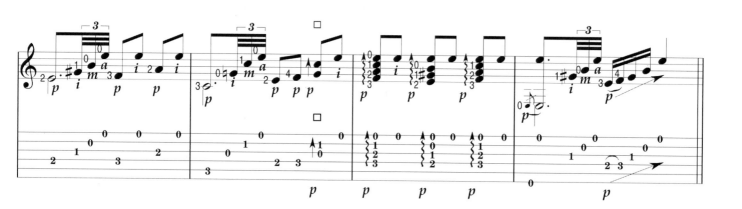

...continues on from 'we can play:'

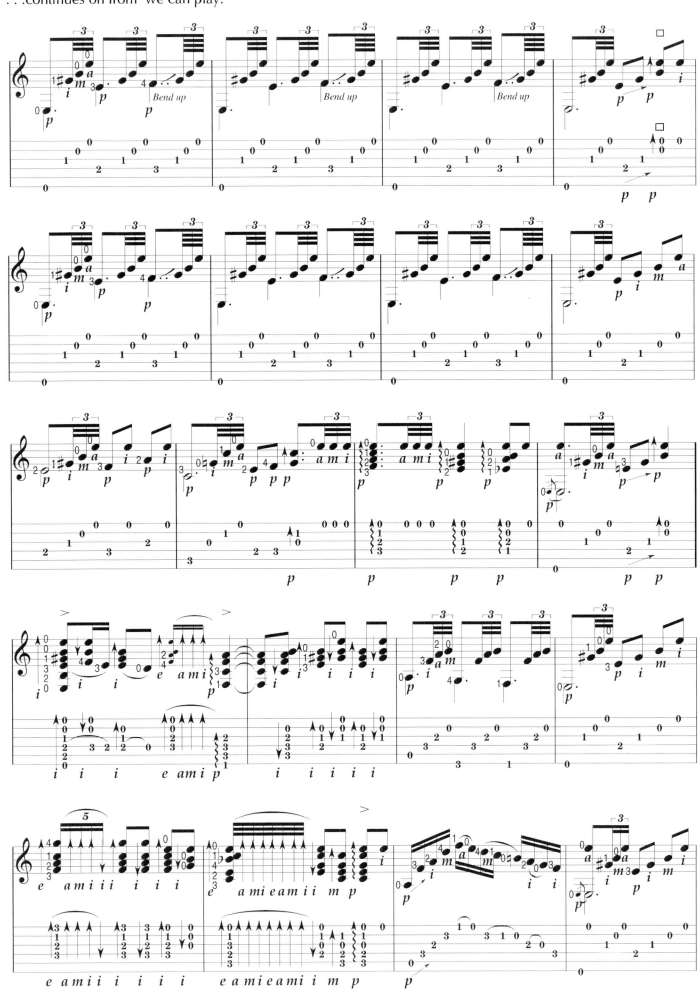

Alzapúa

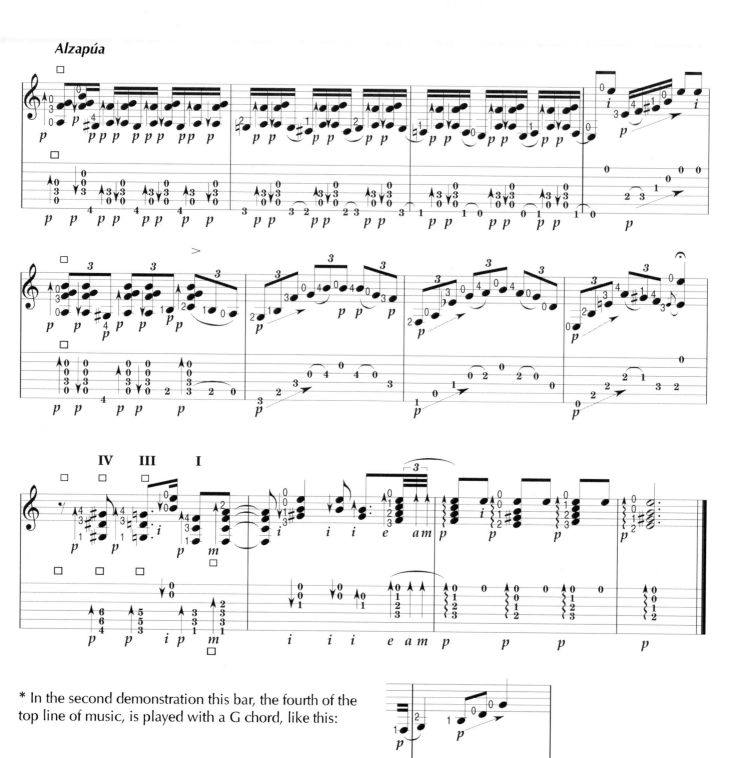

* In the second demonstration this bar, the fourth of the top line of music, is played with a G chord, like this:

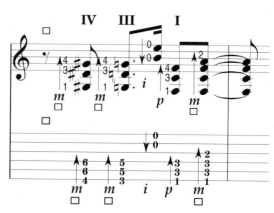

Chapters 64 and 65

BASS-SIDE GOLPES

The *golpe* struck with the middle finger (**m**) of the right hand on the *golpeador* above the bass strings is written with the square symbol underneath the arrow of the stroke. In the first demonstration of the stroke (*above*) just one such *golpe* is played, on the F chord. The three preceding strokes are made with the thumb coinciding with the *golpe*, sounded on the *golpeador* below the treble strings. The second time (as shown on the right), still in Chapter 64, three down-strokes are sounded with the middle finger *golpe* on the *golpeador* above the bass strings. 'Above' and 'below' here refer to the position of the *golpeadores* when the guitar is in the normal playing position. In Chapter 65 there are minor differences: e.g. the thumb-stroke is omitted and the F chord is played earlier, on beat 3.

68

A Simple Falseta

Cejilla al uno
Capo at 1st fret

Cypress flamenco guitar by Hermanos Conde, Madrid, 1995.

A Thumb Falseta

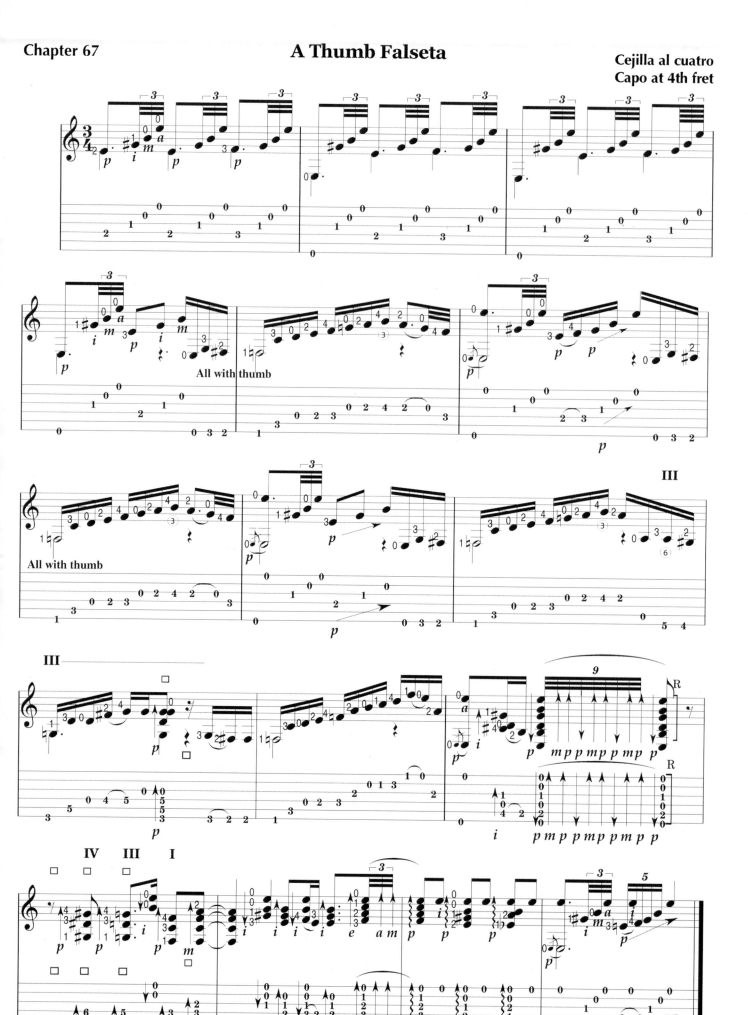

A Repeated-Note Falseta

Cejilla al cuatro
Capo at 4th fret

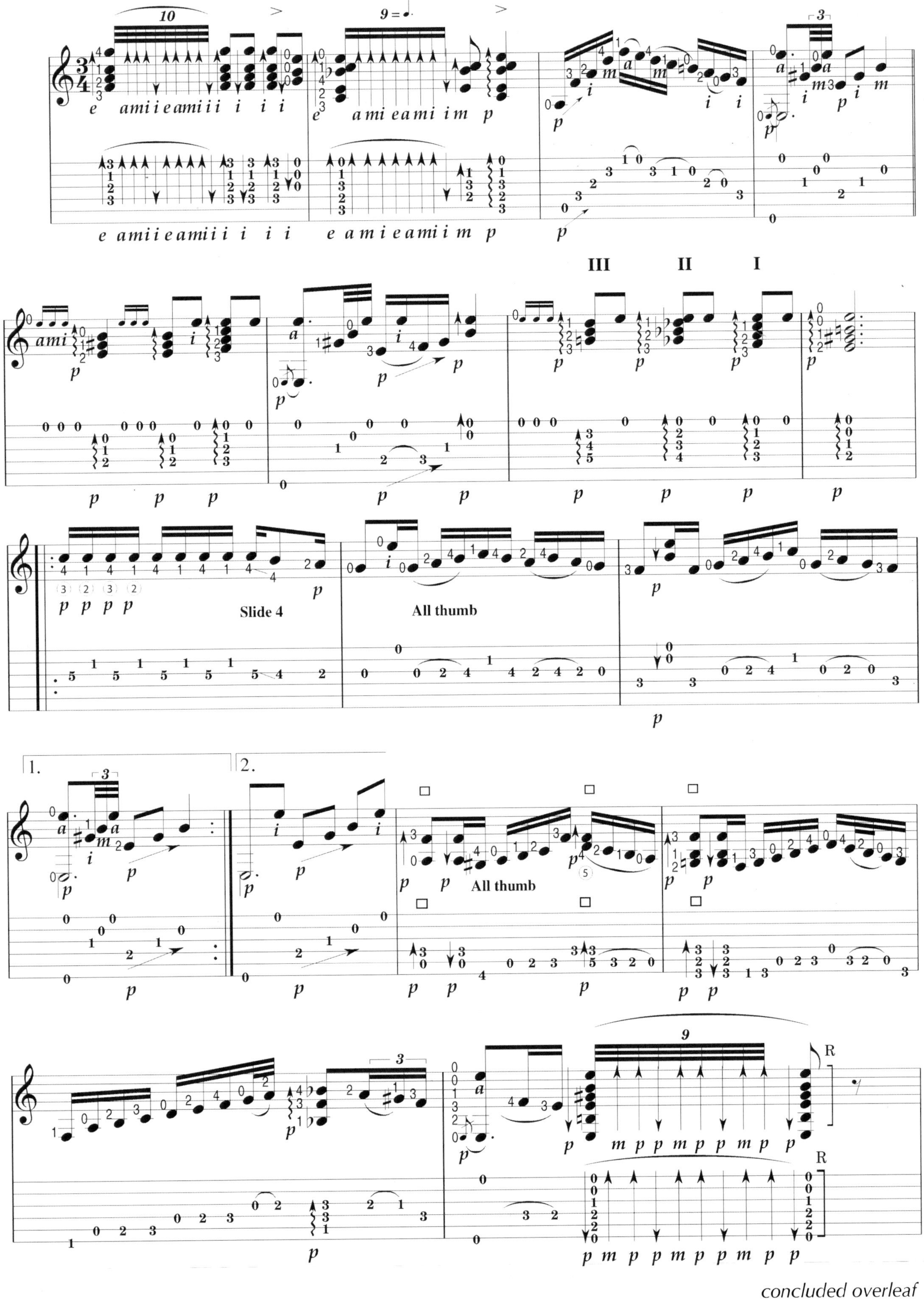

Slide 4

All thumb

All thumb

concluded overleaf

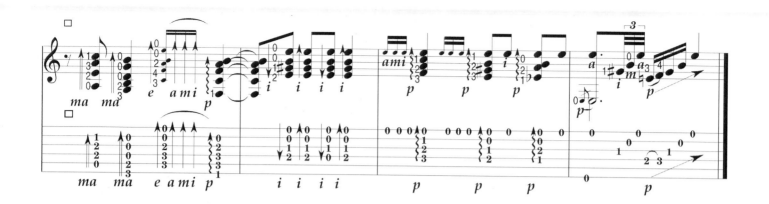

Chapter 69

An Arpegio Falseta

Cejilla al cuatro
Capo at 4th fret

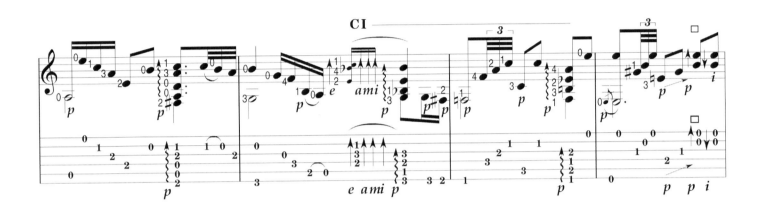

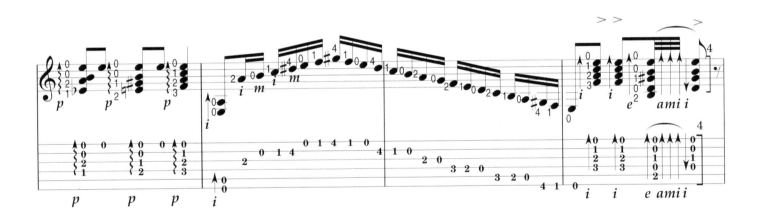

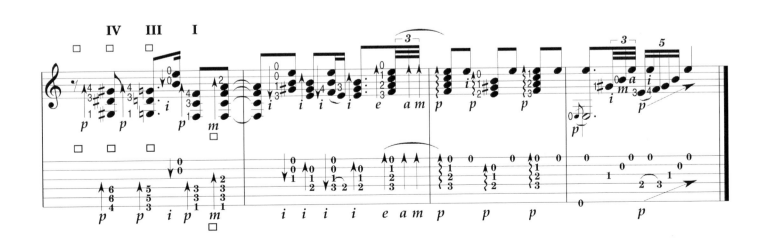

A Wistful Falseta

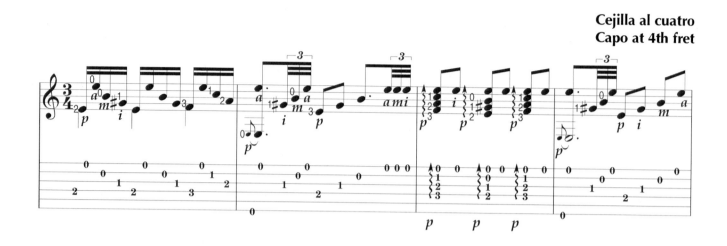

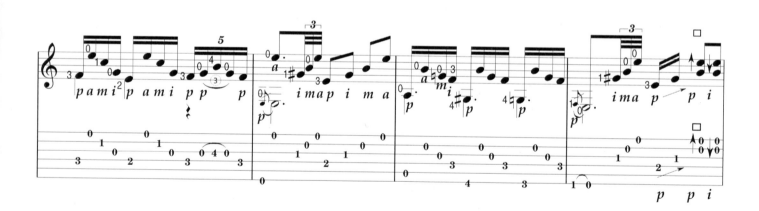

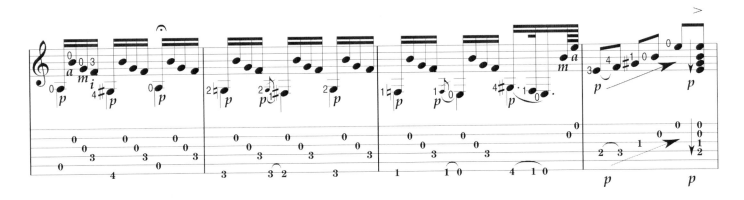

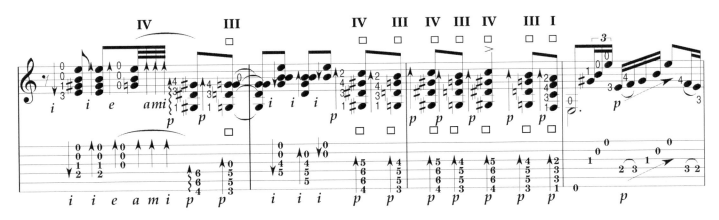

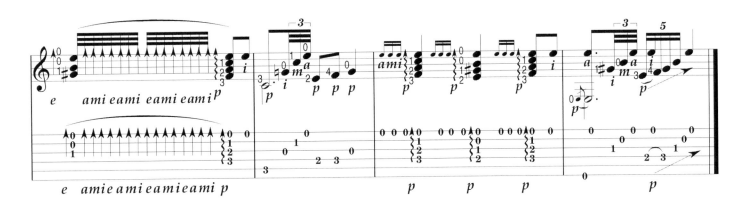

Performing on Spanish TV with Antonio Aparecida, cantaor on the Riquezas album.

A Falseta to Open the Fingers

Cejilla al cuatro
Capo at 4th fret

Another Arpegio Falseta

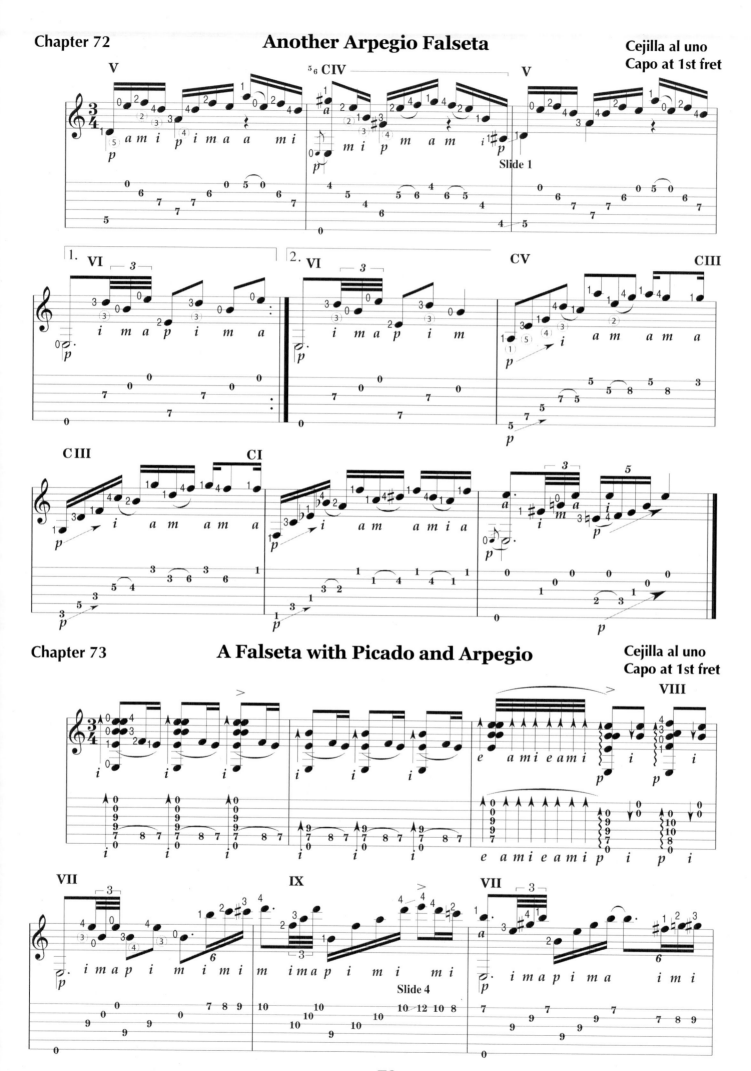

Chapter 73

A Falseta with Picado and Arpegio

Cejilla al uno
Capo at 1st fret

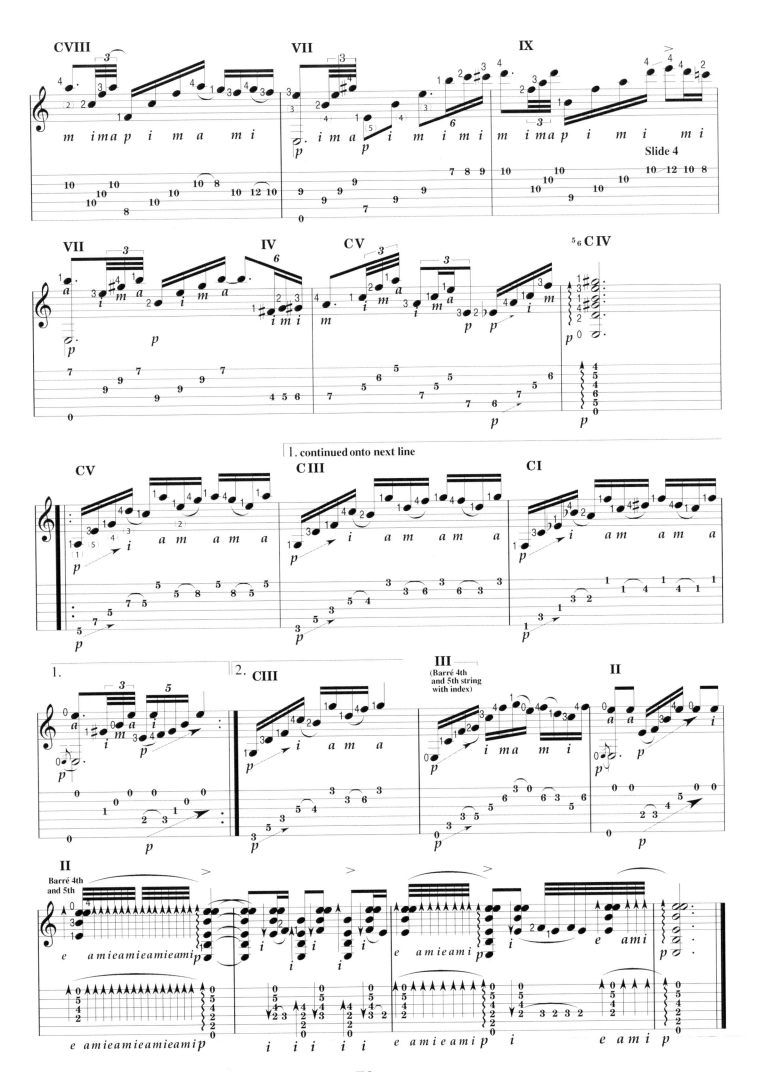

A Trémolo Falseta for Soleá

Cejilla al dos
Capo at 2nd fret

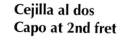

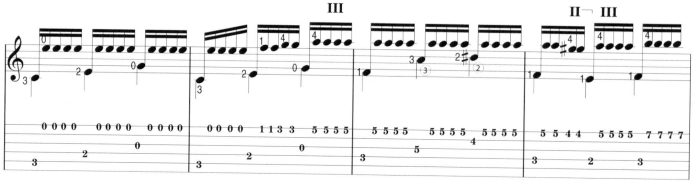

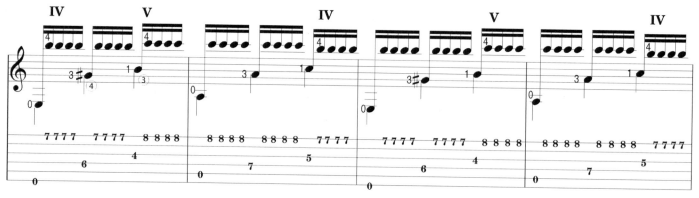

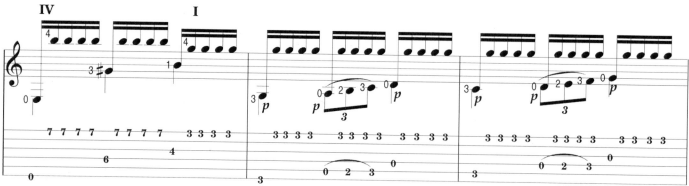

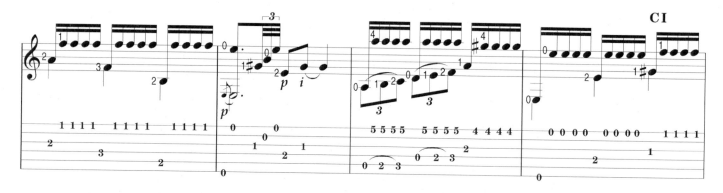

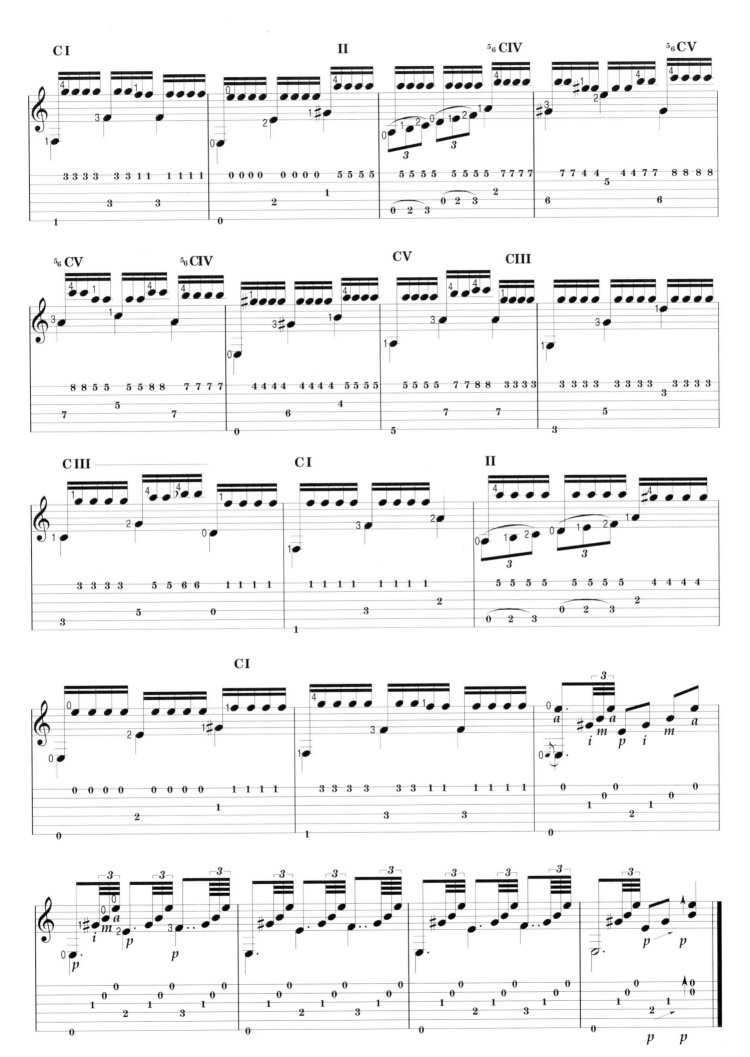

Chapter 76

La Caña

Cejilla al dos
Capo at 2nd fret

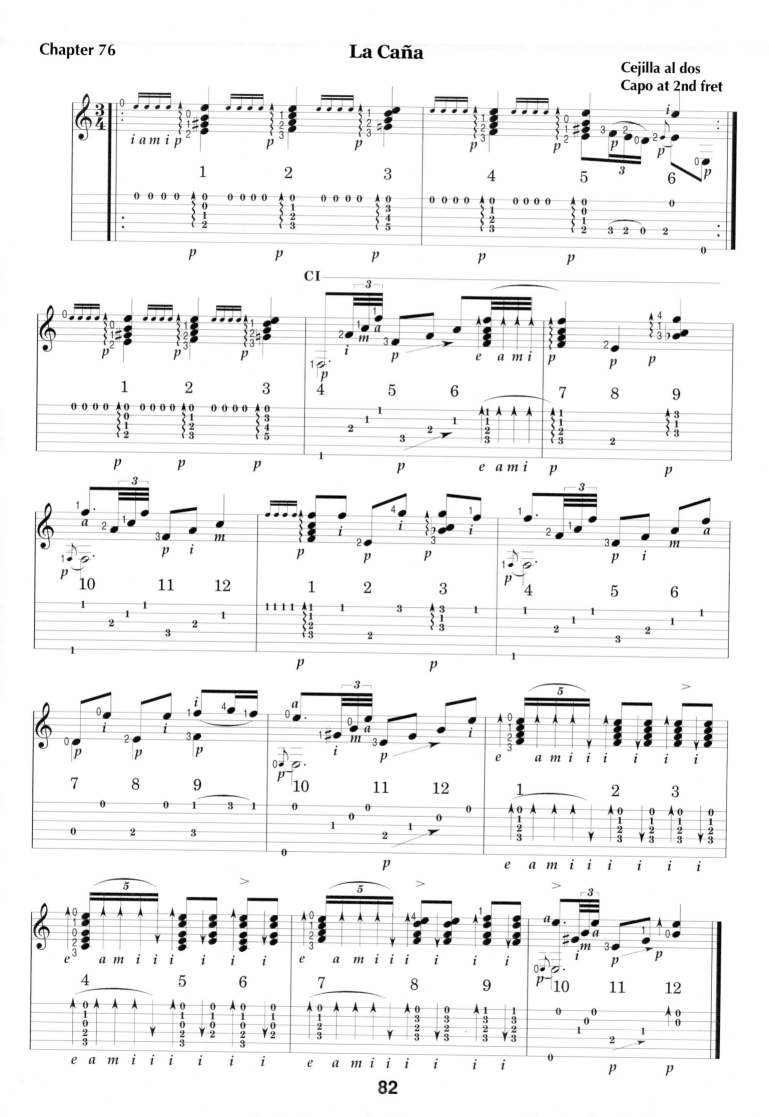

Continuing with a *falseta*:

The following variation gives 'a slightly Arabic sound':

A nice way to resolve before the *falseta* on the following page:

Falseta for La Caña

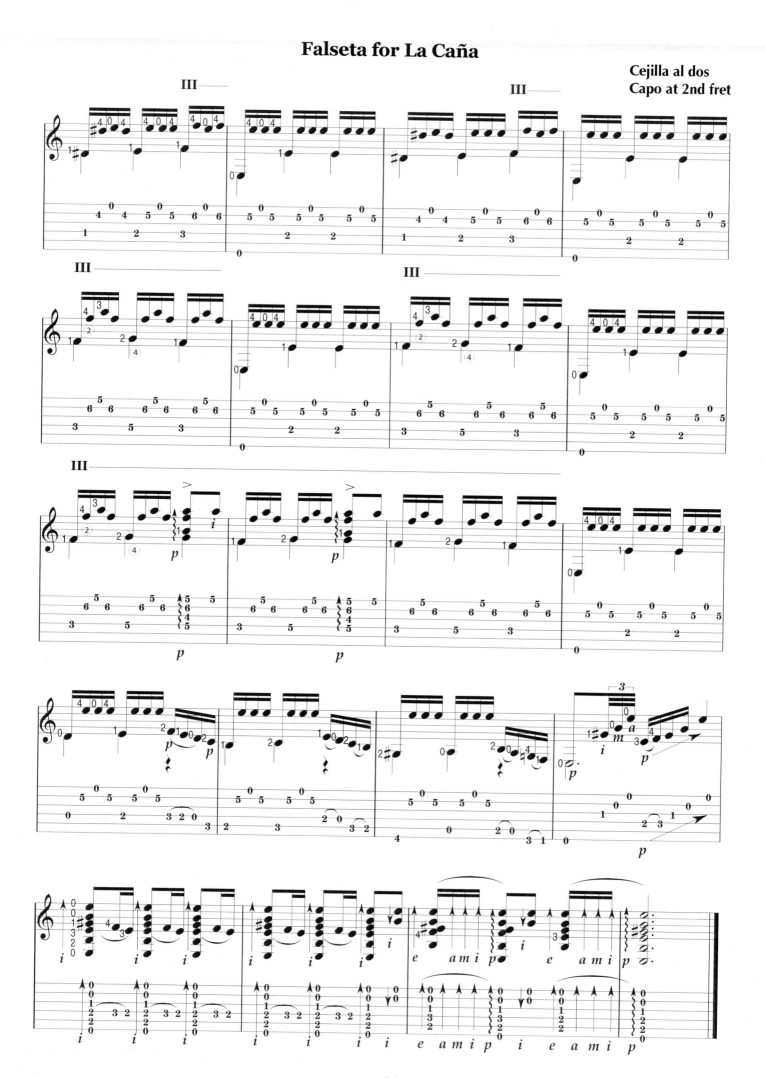

Polo

The transcription is of the second time it is demonstrated.

The first demonstration ends differently:

Soleá *por medio*

More Soleá *por medio*

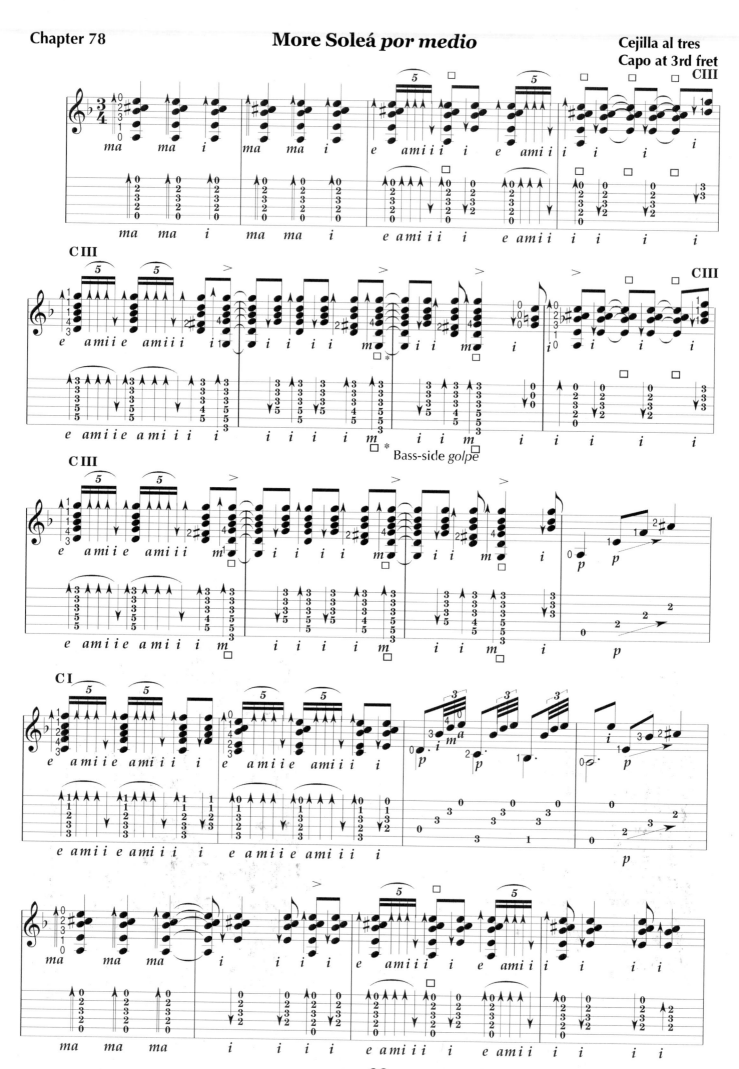

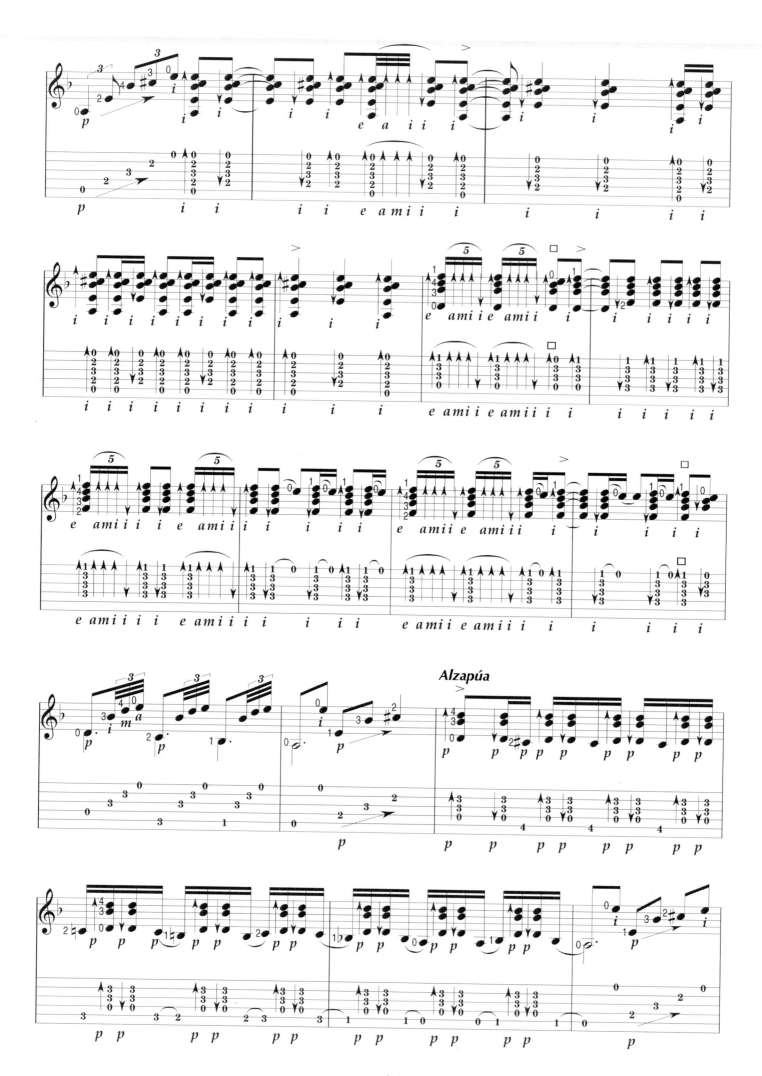

Alzapúa

Performing with dancers Luisa and Miguel.

Alegrías

The basic *compás* of Alegrías is essentially the same as for the Soleá, with a 12-beat *compás* accented on beats 3, 6, 8, 10 and 12. Endings may occur on beat 10.

The emotional tone, the *aire*, however, is very different. *Alegría* means 'happiness' and 'joy' and the *palo* is mostly in a major key, in contrast with the Phrygian-type mode of the Soleá.

The notation of the basic *compás* is again written as four 3-beat bars in 3/4 time:

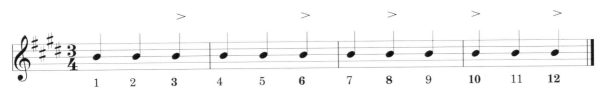

In the first demonstration you will also meet a common syncopation, when the accent on beat 3 is delayed until the half-beat later, beat 3½.

The demonstrations in the DVD (Disc 2) are all in the *por arriba* position of E major, except for the last three sequences before Amparo sings, which are in the A major position (like the *arpegios* demonstrated for the *Escobilla* in the Basic Techniques of Disc 1). The *por arriba* position is the one more commonly used in Alegrías played today.

[The opening *falseta* of the initial dance sequence is transcribed in *Solos Flamencos* Vol.1, p.126]

Soundcheck with guitarist Lolo Jiménez and dancer 'El Tigre'.

Basic Alegrías *por arriba*

Chapter 82

Cejilla al dos
Capo at 2nd fret

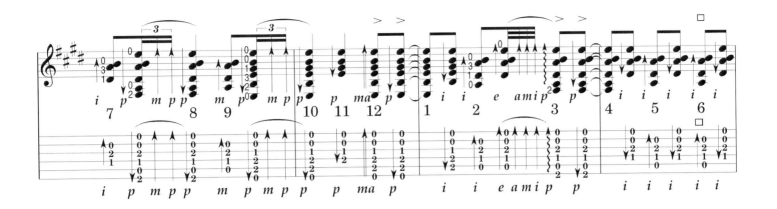

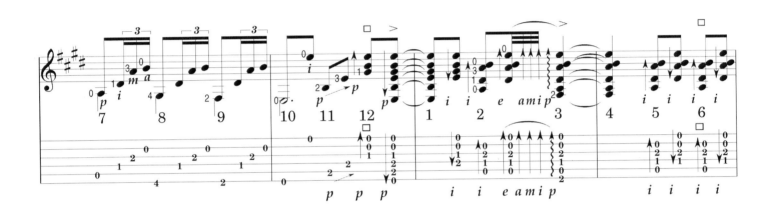

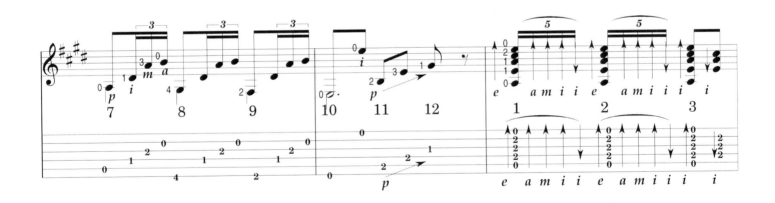

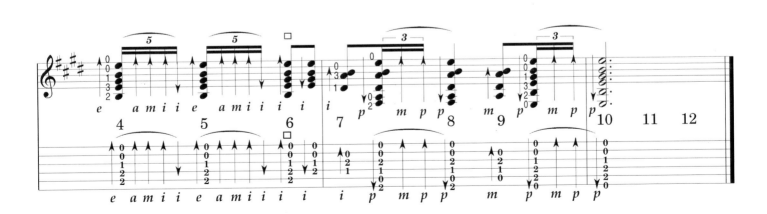

The transcription below is of the first version of the second example of the basic *compás,* after 'so we're talking about . . .'

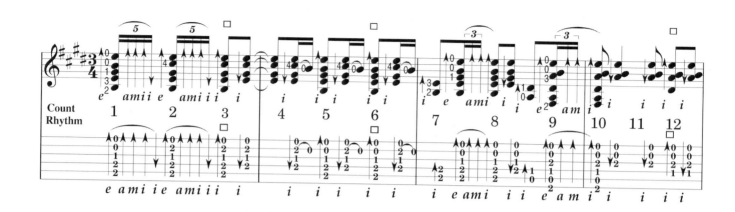

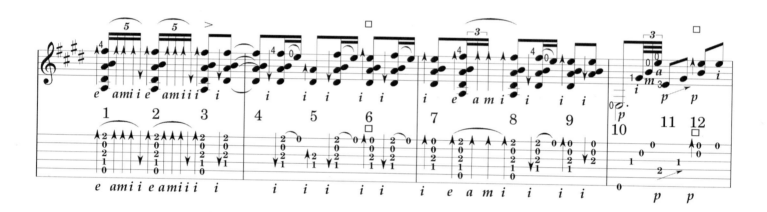

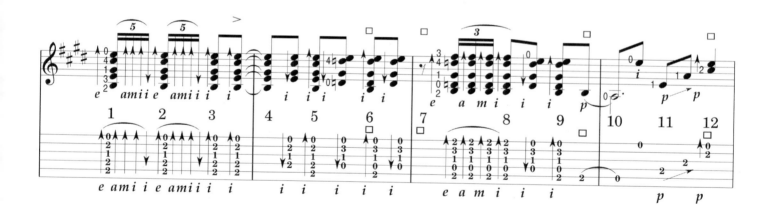

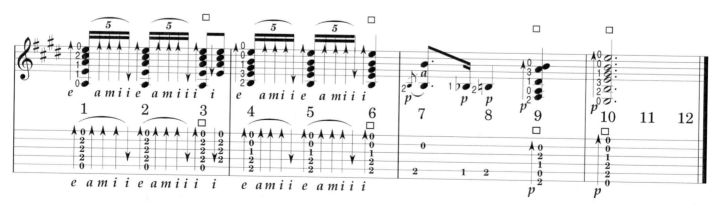

The second, slower version of the above has minor differences. In particular, single 5-note *rasgueos* at the start of each *compás,* followed by an index down- and up-stroke, are played in place of the double five-note *rasgueos* of the above.

Chapter 83

Chords and Ritmeo for Singer

Cejilla al dos
Capo at 2nd fret

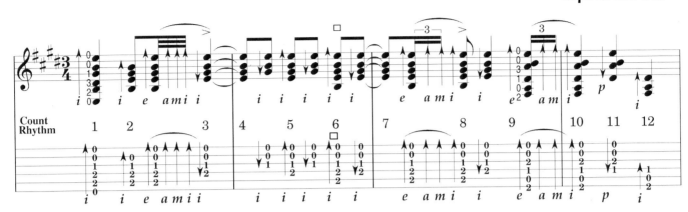

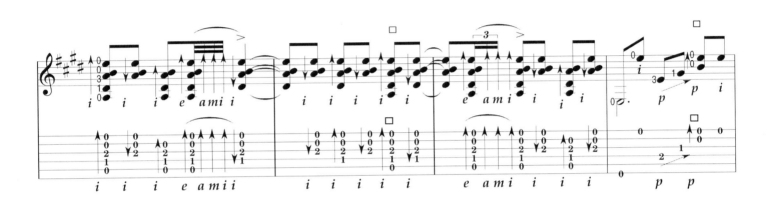

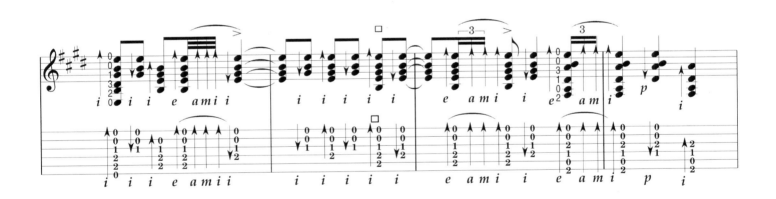

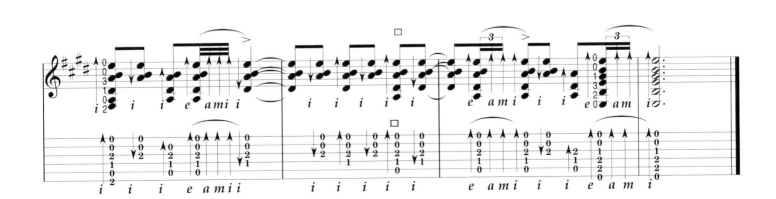

'A More Advanced Form'

Cejilla al dos
Capo at 2nd fret

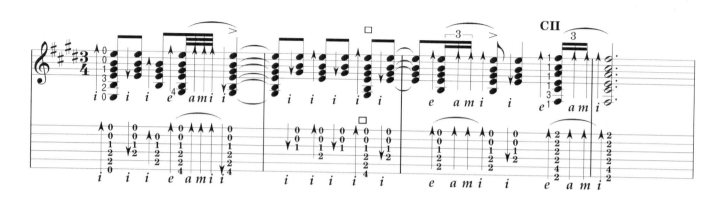

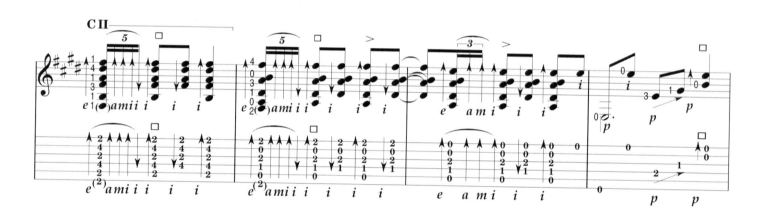

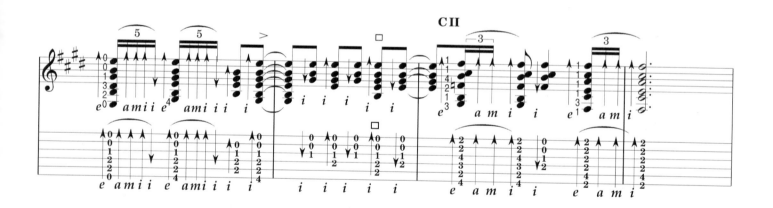

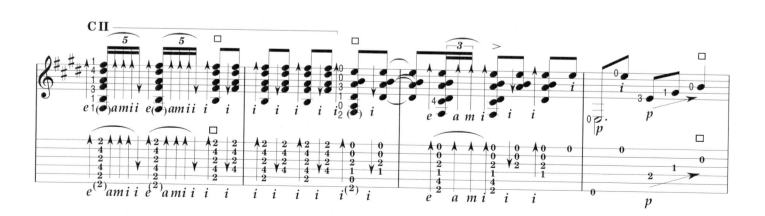

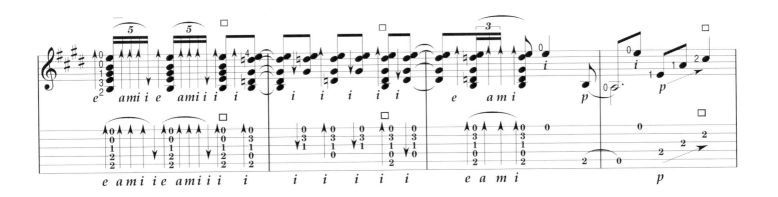

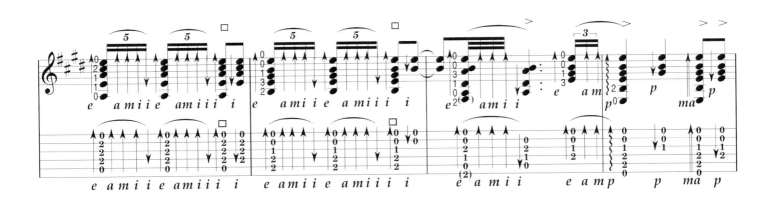

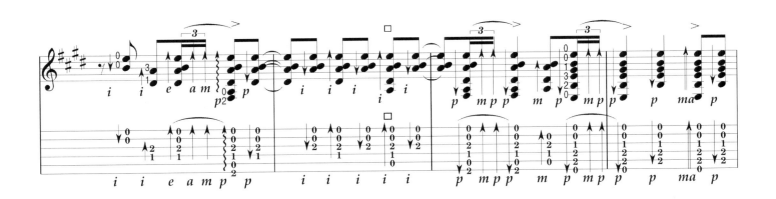

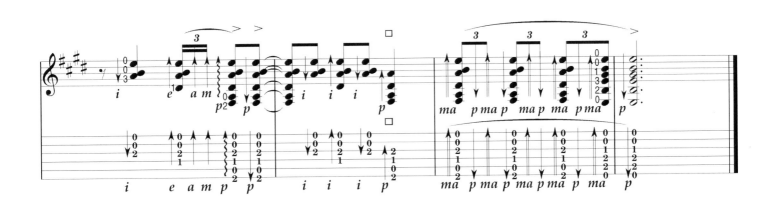

Chapter 84

A Modern Entrada

Cejilla al dos
Capo at 2nd fret

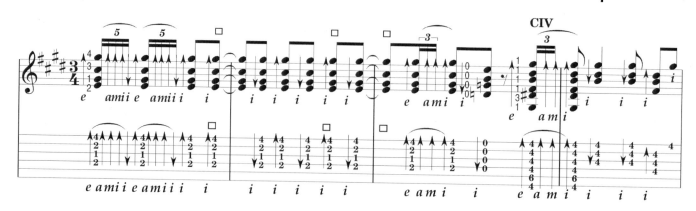

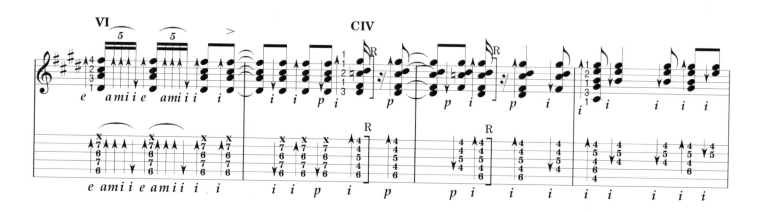

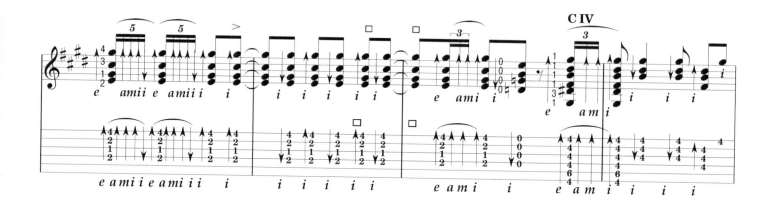

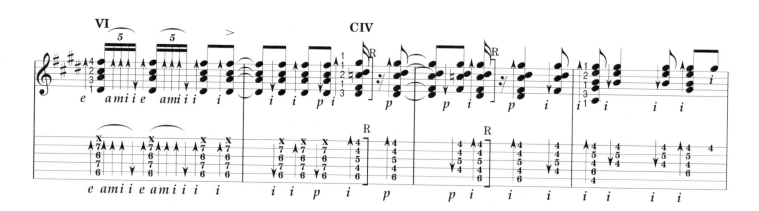

An alternative ending – the transcription is of the fifth demonstration.

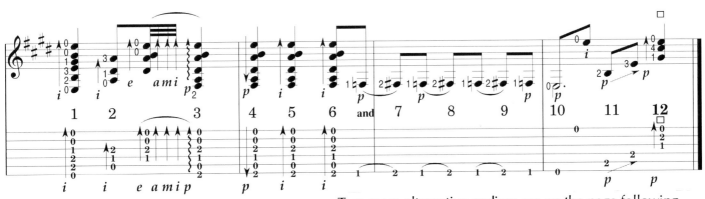

Two more alternative endings are on the page following.

Two more alternative endings

Chapter 87
Subida

Cejilla al dos
Capo at 2nd fret

Chapter 88

Silencio (1st version demonstrated)

Escobilla

The music continues straight on from the previous page. A slower, more detailed demonstration and discussion of the Silencio and Escobilla is given in the video at Chapter 94. The transcription is of the first version at Chapter 89.

In the demonstration at **D2:M3:39**, the above *compás* is played with the *campanela arpegio*.

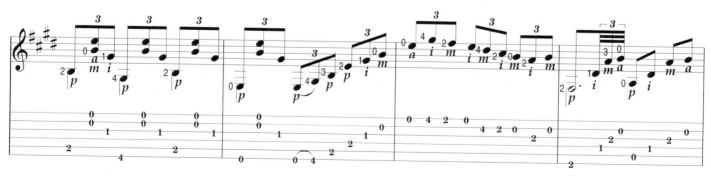

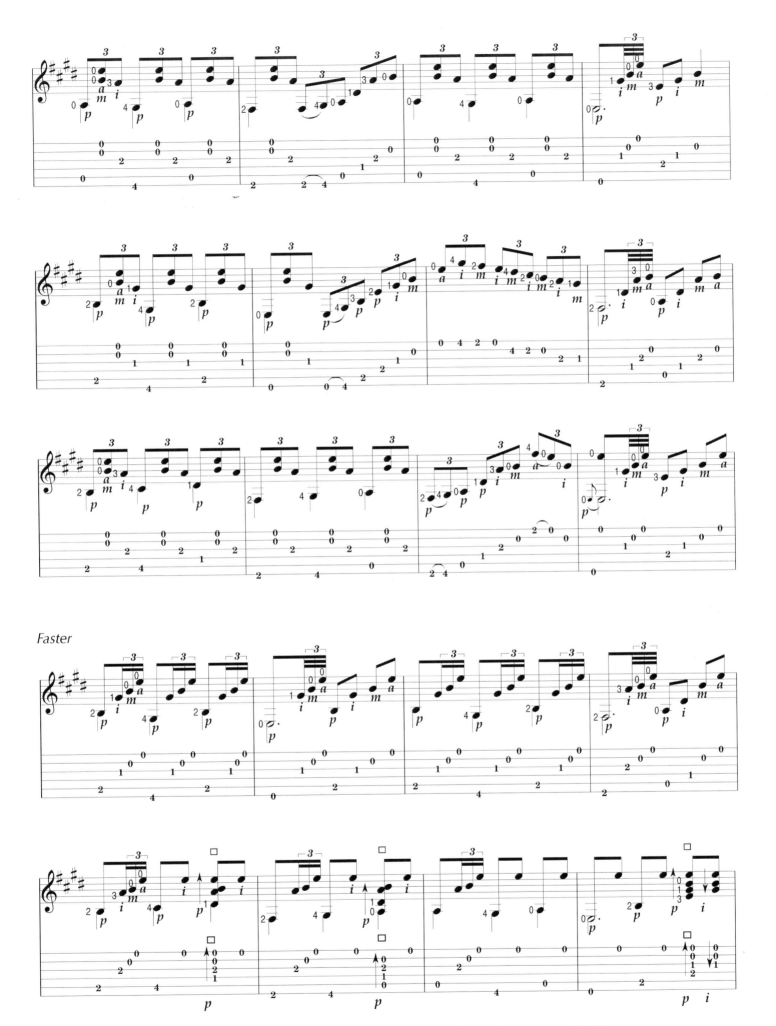

In Chapter 94, the above two 'faster' *compases* are demonstrated with a *golpe* on each third beat.

Chapter 90

The Transition to Bulerías

Cejilla al dos
Capo at 2nd fret

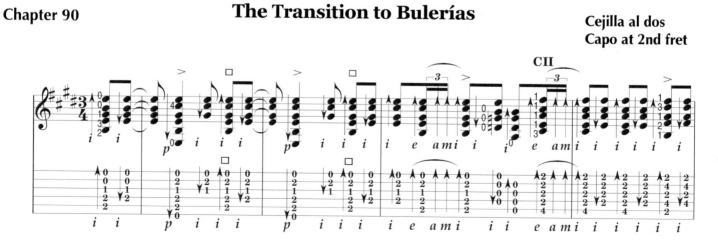

Bulerías Falseta

The transcription is of the first, faster version, continuing from the previous page.

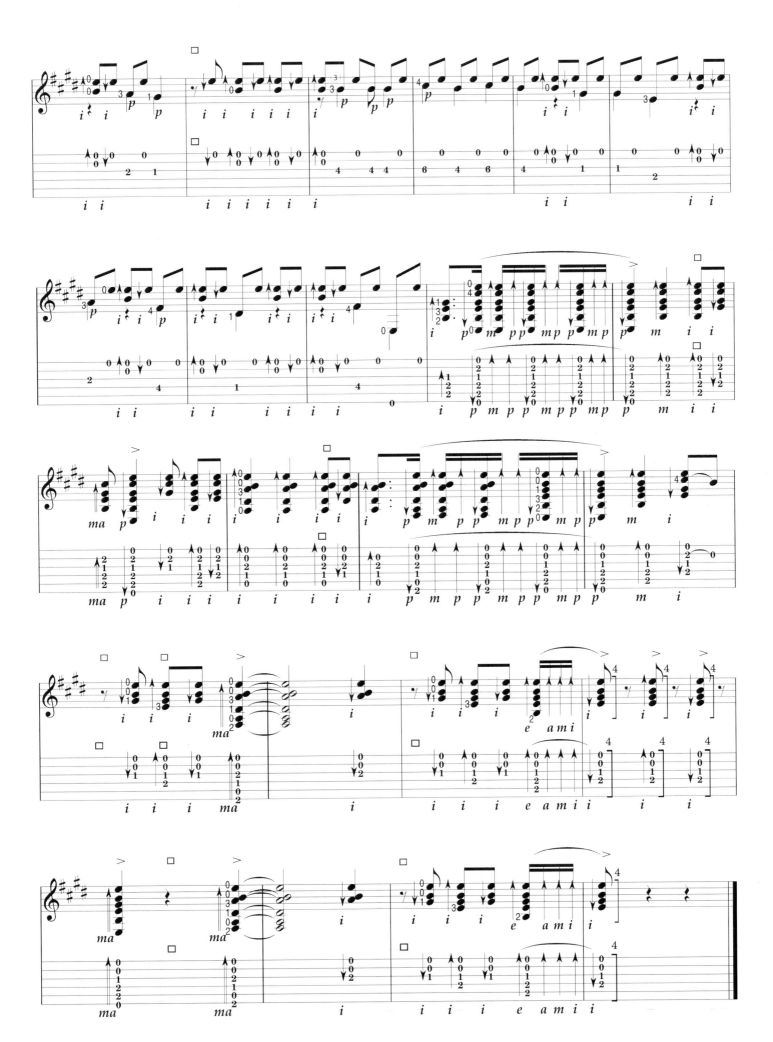

Bulerías de Cádiz (guitar accompaniment)

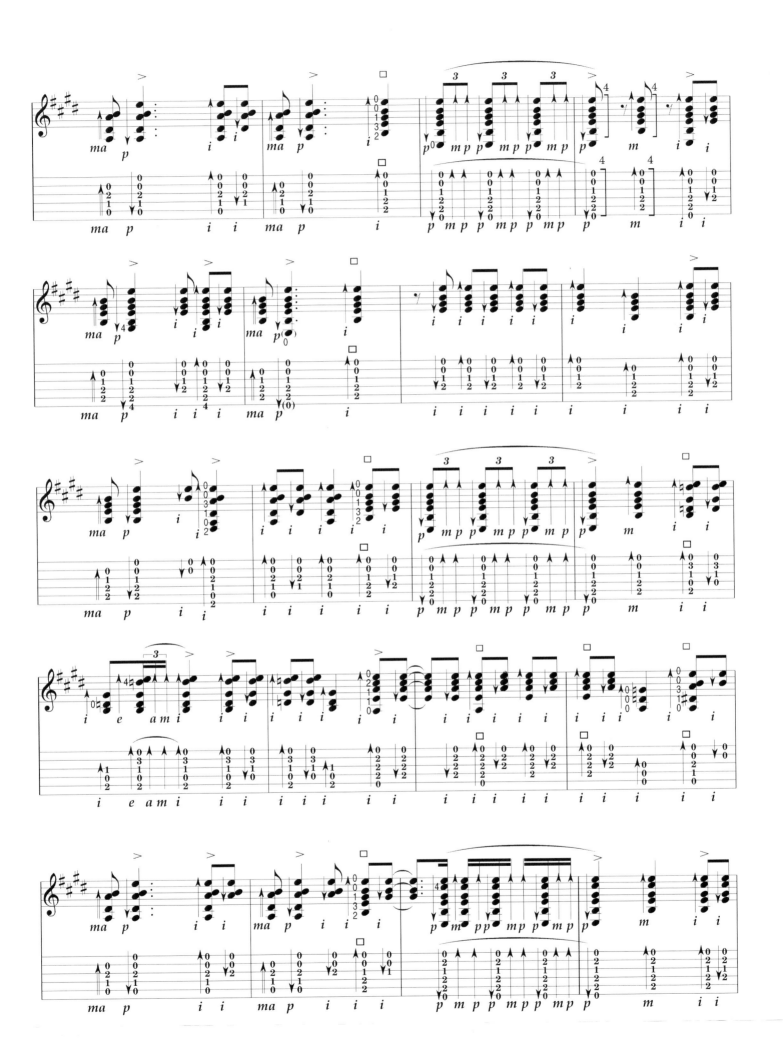

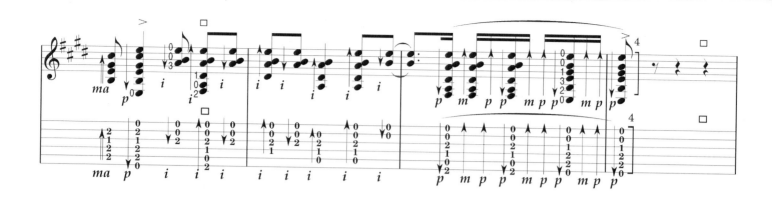

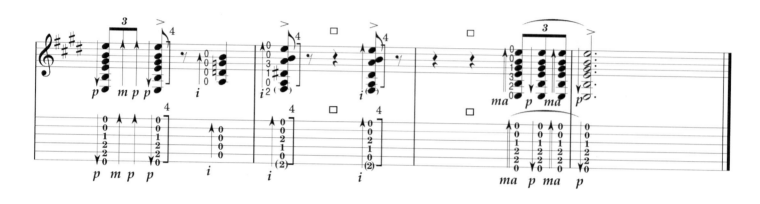

Chapter 95

The Silencio in the Dance

Cejilla al dos
Capo at 2nd fret

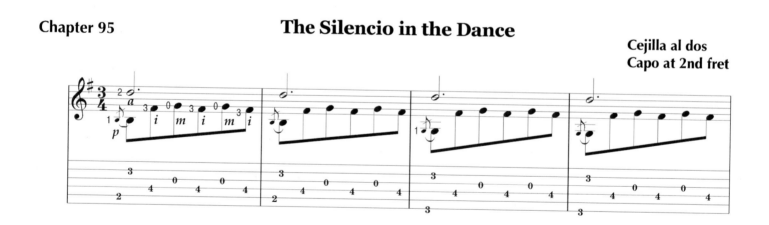

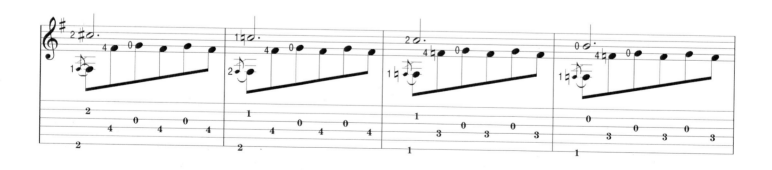

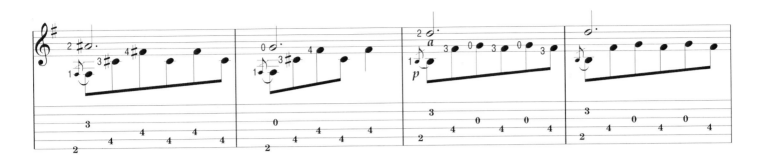

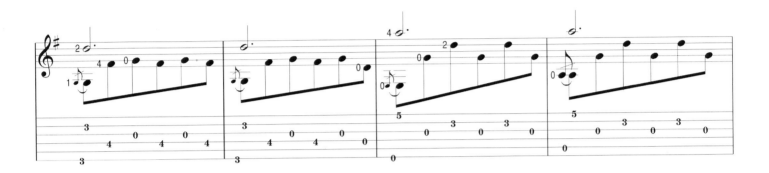

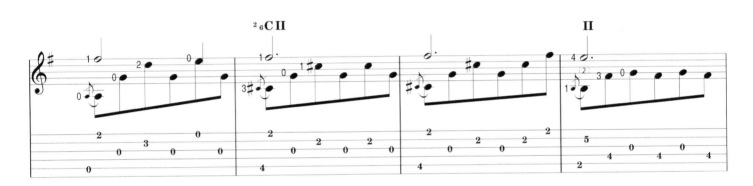

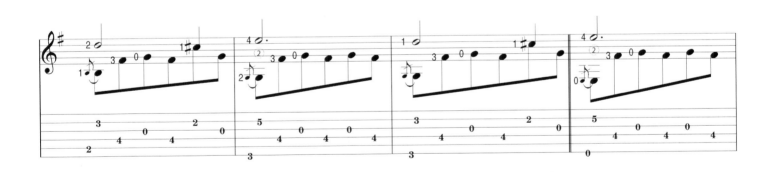

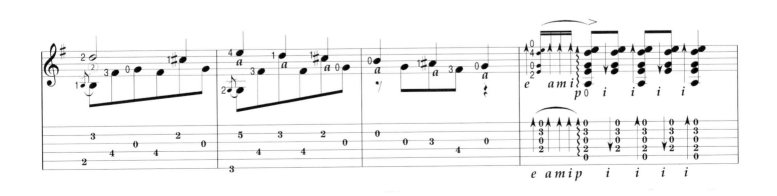

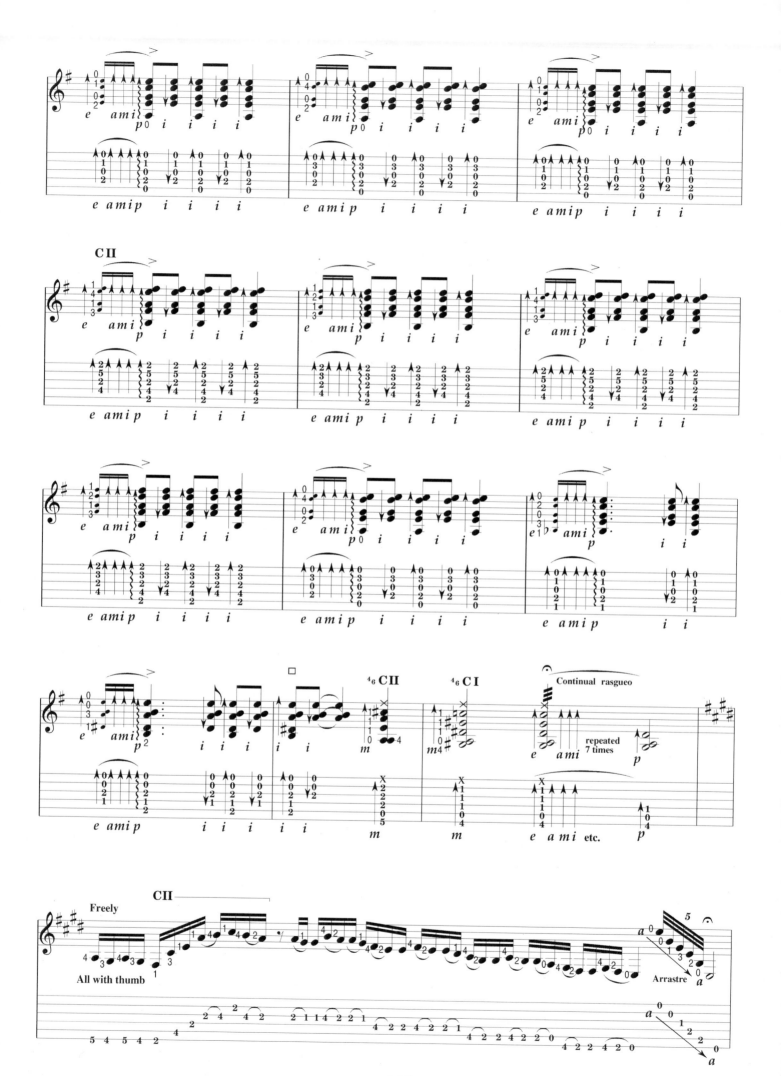

Chapter 96

Falseta A

Cejilla al dos
Capo at 2nd fret

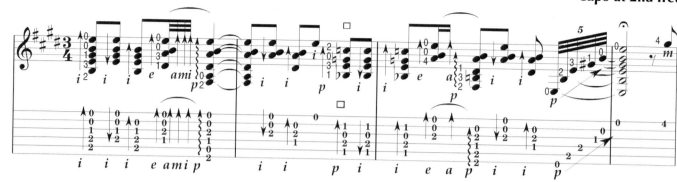

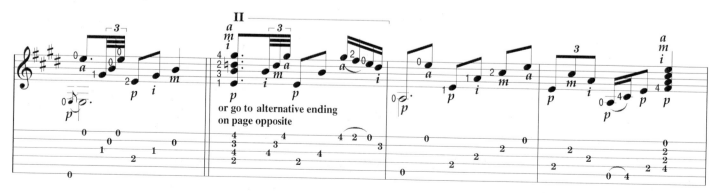

or go to alternative ending
on page opposite

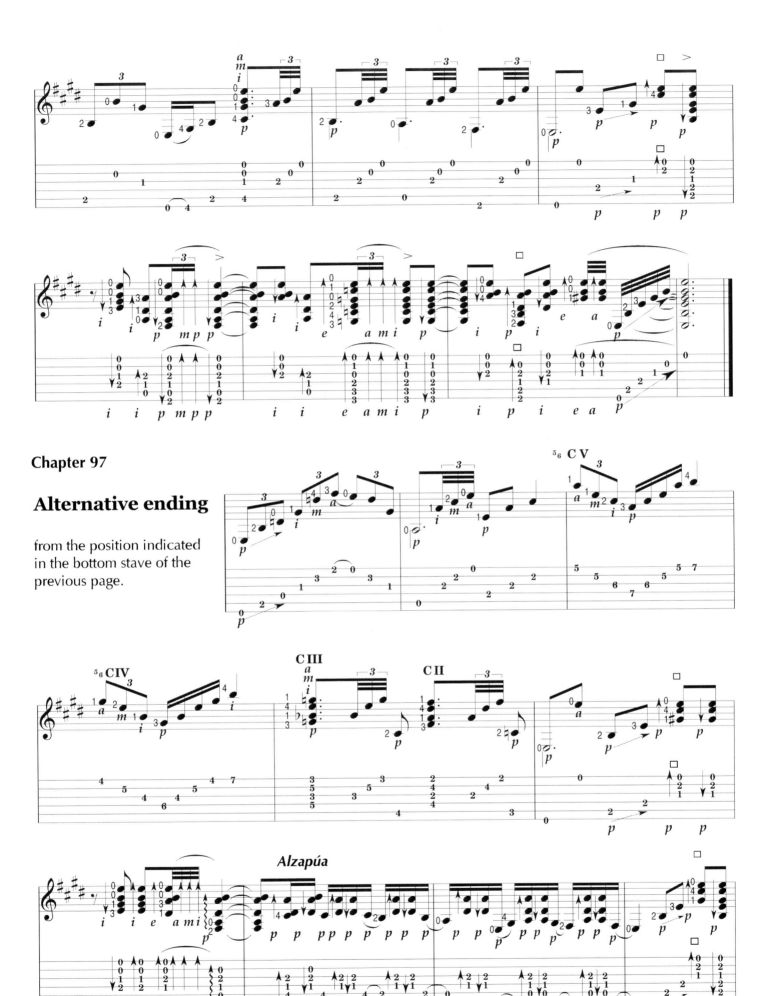

Chapter 97

Alternative ending

from the position indicated
in the bottom stave of the
previous page.

Alzapúa

continued overleaf

Chapter 98

Falseta B

Cejilla al dos
Capo at 2nd fret

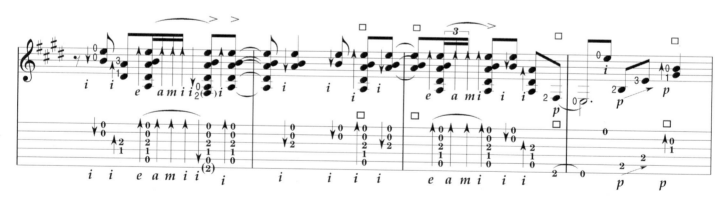

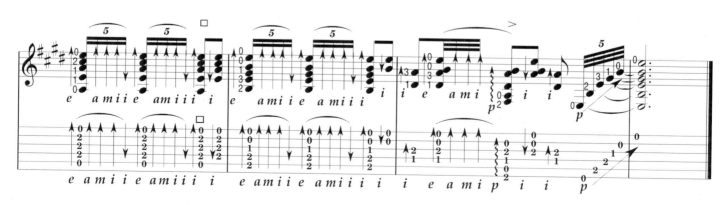

Chapter 99

Trémolo Falseta

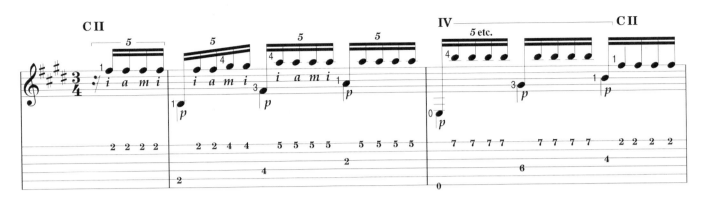

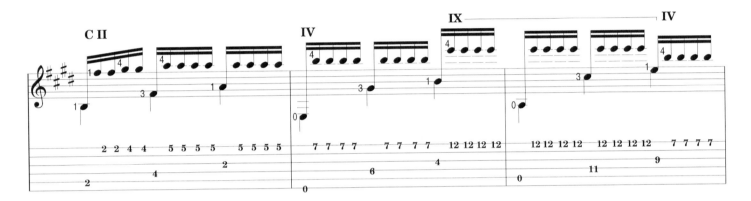

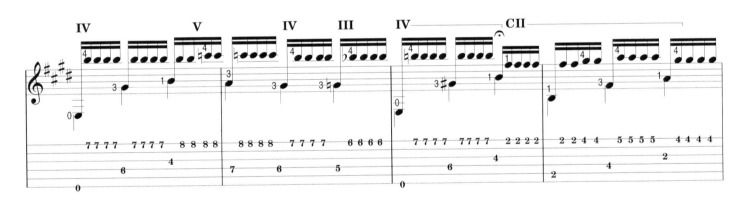

The *falseta* above continues into repeats of *falsetas* A and B.

Chapter 100

Falseta C

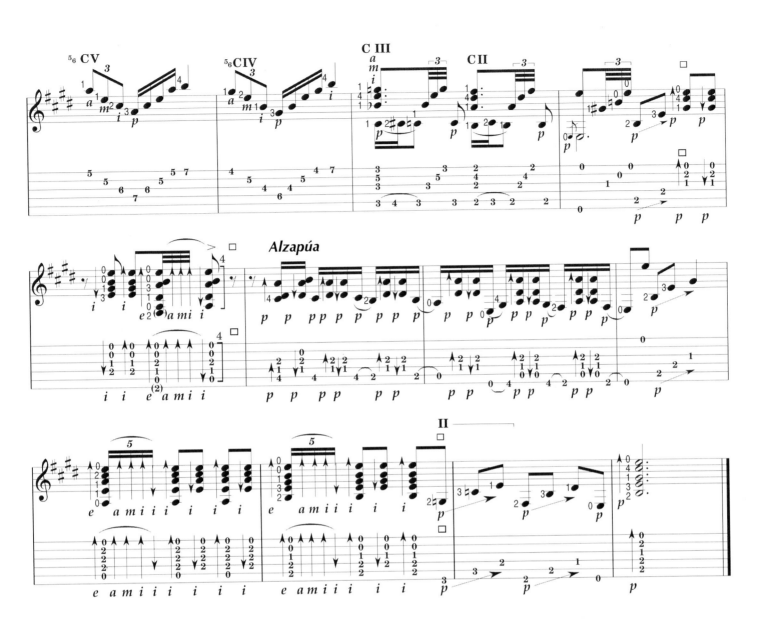

Alzapúa

Chapter 101

Falseta D

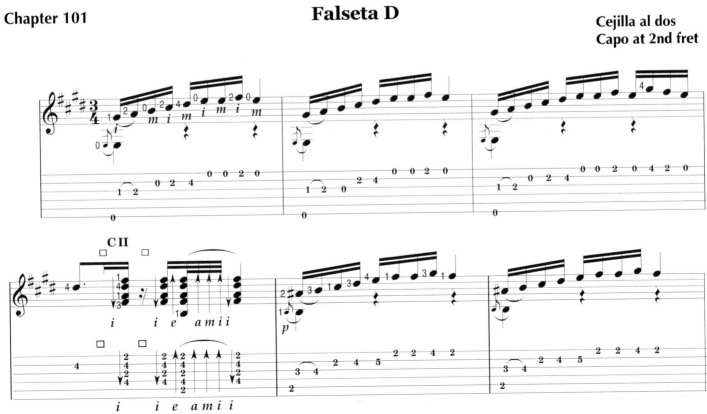

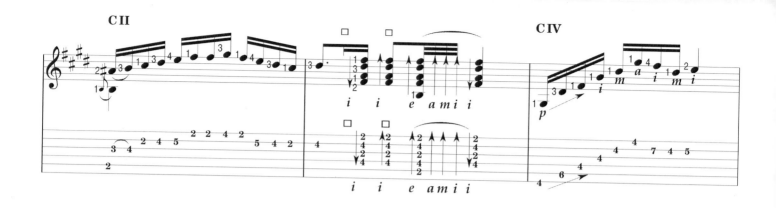

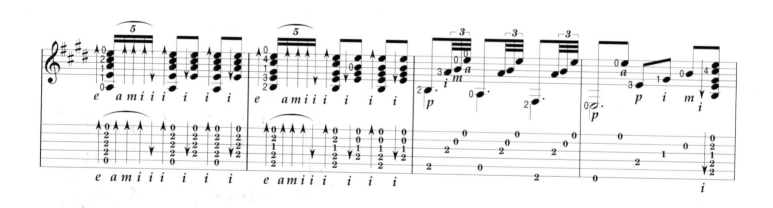

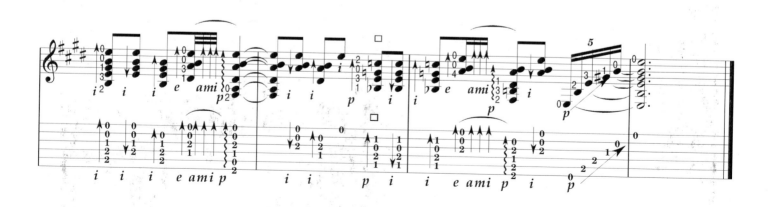

Chapter 102

More Falsetas (Alegrías *por medio*)

Cejilla al dos
Capo at 2nd fret

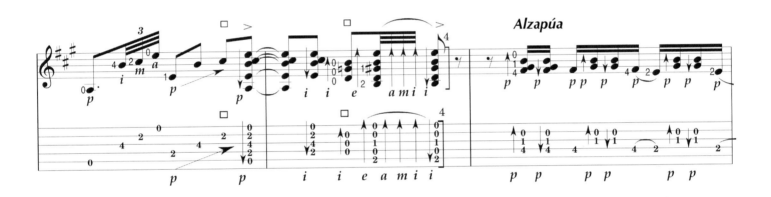

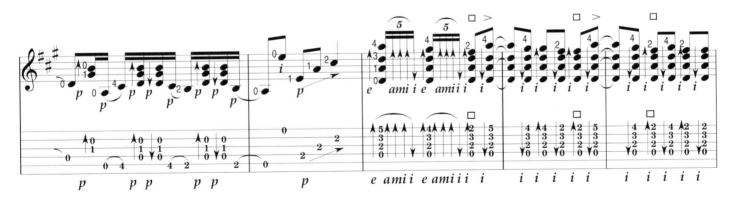

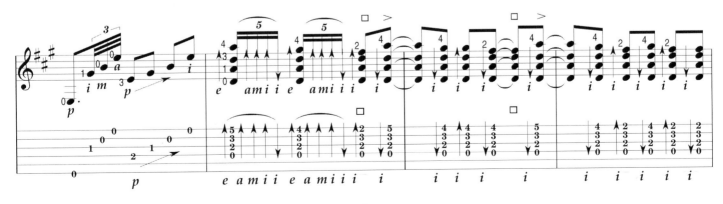

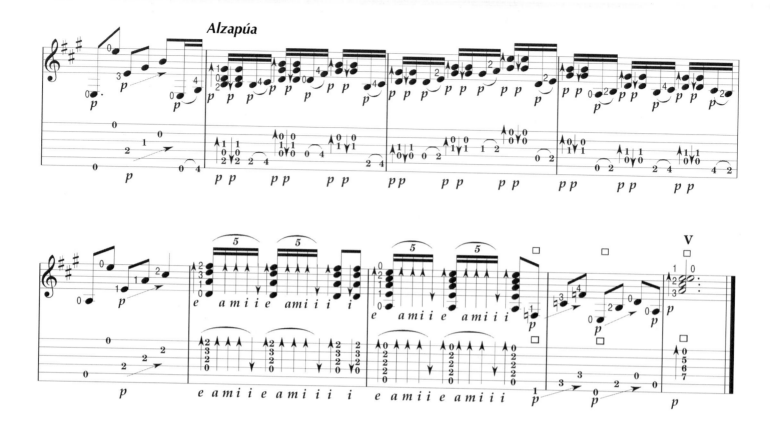

Alzapúa

Juan plays a cypress flamenco guitar of innovative design by the Massachusetts guitar maker Stephan Connor. It has a sound portal facing the player, designed to immerse the player in the sound of the instrument.

Falseta de Niño Ricardo

The *falseta* is here introduced by a *compás* of *rasgueo* which has not been recorded, to show how it starts on the half-beat after beat 11. The transcription is of the first version played.

Cejilla al tres
Capo at 3rd fret

Falseta de Ramón Montoya

1st finger barré across strings 2, 3 and 4

Cejilla al tres
Capo at 3rd fret

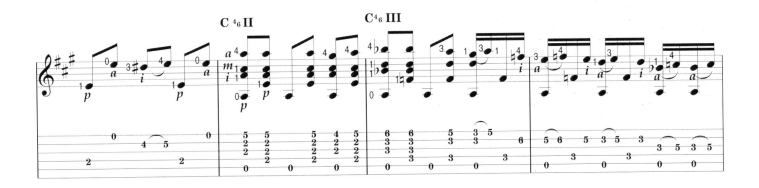

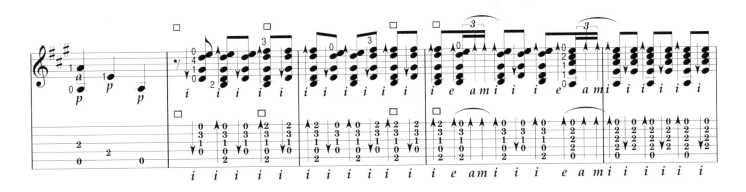

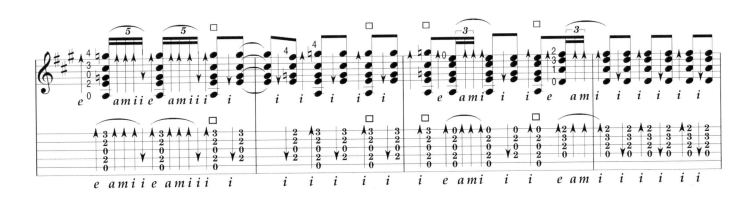

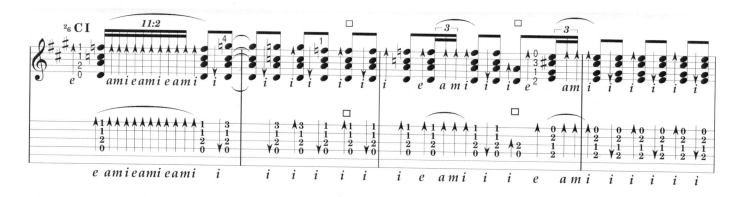

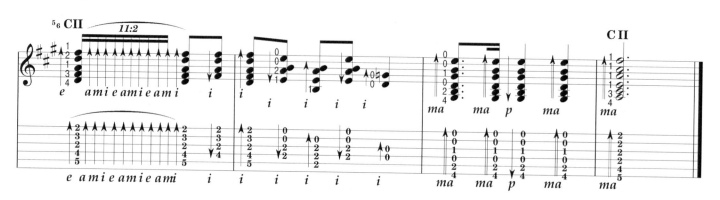

Senior members of the Peña flamenca in Ronda.

Performing in Jersey with Paul Fawcus (flute) and Chris Karan (percussion).

One of the groups at Juan's flamenco guitar course in Ronda (left), at the Reina Victoria Hotel (right), 2012.

ABOUT THE AUTHOR

Juan Martín learned his art in the land of his origin, Málaga, Andalucía. As a teenager, he was chosen by the Spanish film-director German Lorente to play in the film *Donde tú estés*, filmed in Málaga and the Costa del Sol. He is seen playing by the sea in front of the fishing village La Carihuela, where Juan had his home and where he learned so much from visiting artists who would stay in the *pueblo* whilst performing along the coast. Juan practiced his *seguiriyas* with singer 'El Chocolate', his *taranta* with Jacinto Almadén, his *fandangos* with Antonio Canillas and Pepe Palanca, and even Porrina de Badajoz would make an appearance at *El Lago Rojo*, just behind his house, where Juan played in the evenings. Guitarists such as Lorenzo Aparicio from Jerez and Pedro Mancebo, 'Pedrito Sevilla', taught him many secrets of the art of *el toque*. He also got together with local Málaga players like El Niño de Almería, a blind guitarist who would ask Juan along to *El Pimpi*, a famous flamenco venue in Málaga, and Paco de Antequera, a virtuoso who helped Juan hone his technique. Paco was appearing at *El Corral de la Morería,* the prestigious *tablao* in Madrid, and he suggested that Juan was ready to present himself in the capital and mix with some of Spain's greatest players. This happened first through meeting the great Niño Ricardo in the shop of Esteso, the guitar makers, at Calle Gravina 7, and later through visits to Paco de Lucía's home.

He has now recorded 18 albums and performed many hundreds of concerts, solo, with distinguished singers such as the great Rafael Romero, 'El Gallina', and with his groups which have included such outstanding dancers as Eva la Yerbabuena and José Fernández. His method book of 1978 *El Arte Flamenco de la Guitarra* (with audio), widely considered to be a 'bible' of flamenco guitar, is in its eleventh print and has been widely translated. Mel Bay best-sellers include his two volumes of graded *Solos Flamencos*, each with audio and video, which complement this volume. *The Andalucian Suite No.1* book with audio, containing four concert solos from his *Andalucian Suites* album, and *Killer Technique: Flamenco* are also published by Mel Bay.

Juan was invited by Sir Roland Penrose to play for Picasso's 90th birthday celebrations and he has performed in many international festivals, from Hong Kong to Montreux Jazz with Miles Davis and Herbie Hancock and at the First World Guitar Congress in the USA. His tours have taken him around the world from Australia, the U.S.A and Canada to China, the Middle and Far East. In Spain the newspaper *El Mundo* said of him that 'he has a terrifyingly good technique and absolute dominance of the guitar'.

Passionate about communicating the art of flamenco to a wider audience, he tries to find time within his very busy performing schedule to devote time to teaching activities. He has held courses at the Dartington International Summer School and in recent years he has held an annual master-class in Ronda, Andalucía, attended by players from far afield. This series, together with its companion volumes of *Solos Flamencos,* is his most definitive attempt yet to share with aspirant guitarists the distillation of his knowledge and long experience.

Dancer (bailaora) Raquel de Luna.

Singer (cantaora) Amparo Heredia, 'La Repompilla'.

Miguel, Amparo, Raquel and Juan.

JUAN MARTÍN's OTHER PUBLICATIONS

GUITAR MUSIC BOOKS BY JUAN MARTÍN with Patrick Campbell.

KILLER TECHNIQUE: FLAMENCO. (20 pp., Tab only) Mel Bay Publications, Inc.
All the follwing transcriptions in staff notation and guitar tablature (*cifra*).
ANDALUCIAN SUITE No. 1. with audio. Four flamenco guitar solos from the album 'The Andalucian Suites' (FV01). Mel Bay Publications, Inc. Previous edition published by IMP, International Music Publications Ltd, Southend Road, Woodford Green, Essex IG8 8HN, UK.
JUAN MARTÍN's GUITAR METHOD: EL ARTE FLAMENCO DE LA GUITARRA
with 60-minute audio recording. United Music Publishers (UMP), 33 Lea Road, Waltham Abbey, Essex EN9 1ES, UK. Distributed in USA in two-volume edition by Theodore Presser.
THE EXCITING SOUND OF FLAMENCO. Volumes 1 and 2, each containing two solos from Argo album of the same name. United Music Publishers Limited.

GUITAR MUSIC WITH VIDEOS BY JUAN MARTÍN with Patrick Campbell

PLAY FLAMENCO GUITAR WITH JUAN MARTÍN: SOLOS FLAMENCOS. With/*con* **video** and/*y* **audio**. Text in English and Spanish. **VOLUME/*TOMO* 1**. Grades/*Niveles* 0 - 5. 42 Solos. **VOLUME/*TOMO* 2**.
Grades/*Niveles* 6 - 8. 21+ Solos. Mel Bay Publications, Inc.
LEARN FLAMENCO GUITAR WITH JUAN MARTÍN: LA GUITARRA FLAMENCA, with video. Six half-hour video lessons fully transcribed into staff notation and tab (*cifra*) in 188-page book. Faber Music Ltd., Burnt Mill, Elizabeth Way, Harlow, CM20 2HX, UK. Previous edition published on video-cassette, then DVDs, with music booklets by Warner/Chappell Music Ltd.

VHS VIDEO OF JUAN MARTÍN's FLAMENCO DANCE COMPANY FROM SEVILLA

LIVE AT THE BARBICAN (London) 1992 recording of Juan Martín's Flamenco Dance Company. 2+ hours.

DVDs

JUAN MARTÍN: LIVE IN LONDON. Double DVD filmed at the Barbican in 2009. Flamencovision.com
THE FOUR MARTINS with Martin Simpson, Martin Carthy, Martin Taylor. P3 MUSIC DVD-10
JUAN MARTÍN & HIS FLAMENCO DANCE COMPANY. Open-air performance in Istanbul. 1 hr. 39 mins.
Mel Bay Publications, Inc.

ALBUMS RECORDED BY JUAN MARTÍN.

CDs, LPs, cassettes, most recent listed first.
JUAN MARTÍN y RAFAEL ROMERO 'El Gallina' 8 tracks, including 4 historic recordings from 1978. CD FV13
JUAN MARTÍN: SOLO Remastered selection. CD FV12
JUAN MARTÍN with the Royal Philharmonic Orchestra: SERENADE Flamencovision FV11 remastered edition, with 5 bonus tracks. Originally published as WEA and K-Tel NE 1267 (Europe), P1146 (Warner-Pioneer Corporation, Japan)
EL EMBRUJO DE LA GUITARRA 3CDs with 6 tracks by Juan Martín. Others by Paco de Lucía, Manolo Sanlúcar, Andrés Batista, Niño de Pura. Divucsa, Spain, 310971,2 and 3.
JUAN MARTÍN: RUMBAS ORIGINALES Flamencovision FV10
JUAN MARTÍN y su compañía flamenca: LIVE en directo. 2 CDs. Flamencovision FV09
JUAN MARTÍN: CAMINO LATINO with Flora Purim, Alberto Moreira and others. CD FV08
JUAN MARTÍN and ANTONIO APARECIDA cantaor flamenco: **RIQUEZAS** CD FV07
JUAN MARTÍN: EL ALQUIMISTA The Alchemist. Flamencovision CD FV06
JUAN MARTÍN: ARTE FLAMENCO PURO Flamencovision CD FV05
JUAN MARTÍN: MUSICA ALHAMBRA Flamencovision CD FV04
PICASSO PORTRAITS digitally remastered. Flamencovision CD (or CC) FV03
RETRATO A PICASSO Divucsa 31-837. Previously published by POLYDOR 1st edition: POLD5048, 2nd ed.
SPELKP 70
LUNA NEGRA Flamencovision CD (or CC) FV02 (edición española: Divucsa)
THE ANDALUCIAN SUITES I - IV Flamencovision CD (or CC) FV01
LAS SUITES DE ANDALUCÍA Divucsa CD 5616
THROUGH THE MOVING WINDOW RCA- BMG PK833036 (Europe) RCA- BMG 3036-NOVUS (USA)
PAINTER IN SOUND WEA and KTEL NE 1320 (UK); 3005-1-N (USA)
Also: **LA MÚSICA DE LAS PINTURAS** WEA (Madrid) 240748
THE SOLO ALBUM WEA WX17
ROMANCE with Orchestra. EMI THIS 26 - 0037
¡OLÉ DON JUAN! - FLAMENCO EN ANDALUCÍA EMI NTS 126
THE FLAMENCO SOUL OF JUAN MARTÍN DECCA (UK) SKL 5256
THE EXCITING SOUND OF FLAMENCO ARGO (Division of Decca UK) ZDA 201